# What It Takes:

# The Secrets of Becoming a Successful Trader

by Russ "Eddie Z" Hazelcorn

Printed in the United States of America

10 9 8 7 6 5 4 3 2 1

Hazelcorn, Russ, 1969 -

What It Takes: The Secrets of Becoming a Successful Trader / Russ Hazelcorn, Eddie Z.

p. cm.

ISBN-13 978-1518722950; ISBN-10 1518722954 (pbk)

1. Floor traders (Finance) – United States – Interviews. 2. Stockbrokers – United States – Interviews. 3. Investment advisers – United States – Interviews. I. Z, Eddie. II. Hazelcorn, Russ. III. Title.

# Dedication

For Ivonhe, the love of my life.

# Contents

# Acknowledgements

I am sincerely grateful to the following people, who contributed to making this book possible: Matt DeYoung, Roberto Pedone, Markus Heitkoetter, Doc Severson, Todd Mitchell, Nigel Hawkes, Norman Hallett and Rob Booker.

I'd also like to thank my staff, who puts up with me on a daily basis: Adam Fink, Ashlee Hasemeyer, Lawrance Courtney, Gene Fox, Joey Shakespeare and Ivonhe Mantilla.

Lastly, I would like to thank my dad, Howard Hazelcorn.

# About The Author

Eddie Z. is a full-time day trader, educator, and total computer geek. He is also the founder of EZ Trading Computers (EZTradingComputers.net), the industry leader in high-powered trading computers for traders of all markets. Eddie founded EZ Trading Computers to achieve a single goal: "to educate fellow traders on trading technology, and to offer them the highest quality computers at the lowest possible prices with the best customer service."

Besides his love of technology, Eddie has over 28 years of full-time experience trading the markets. He is the creator of EZBreakouts.com, an educational website focused on teaching traders exactly how to day trade and swing trade US equities. Eddie's unique teaching style incorporates both a bottom-up and top-down approach. Eddie offers step-by-step instruction (the bottom-up method), and provides his own list of 10 stocks that have an extremely high probability of moving higher the next day. Students are encouraged to reverse engineer the list (the top-down method). This unique teaching style results in a much higher student rate of success.

Eddie has had a lifetime of experience in the financial markets. Eddie's father was a commodities future trader on the New York Mercantile Exchange (NYMEX). From the time he was five years old, his father would take him to work. Even in the 70s, before computerized trading, Eddie was mesmerized by all the people huddled in the trading pit, screaming and getting very carried away. Interest in trading started in his teens, when his dad taught him how to draw point-and-figure charts, by hand, with pencil and graph paper. His first full-time job on Wall Street started in 1987 on the floor of the NYMEX, the very first Monday after he graduated high school.

In the 90s and 2000s, Eddie had a 17-year career as a licensed stockbroker. Now he enjoys trading his own accounts exclusively. He holds an undergraduate degree in accounting from Penn State and an MBA from Lehigh University, but he attributes real-world, in-the-trenches experience to some of his greatest learning.

# Introduction

Thanks for reading this book! *What It Takes: The Secrets of Becoming a Successful Trader* is a priceless collection of personal stories, anecdotes, experiences, and trading insights from several trading masters of Wall Street. This collection of experiences represents over 150 combined years of full-time dedication to studying, understanding and mastering the markets.

As a veteran or new trader, you may be asking yourself: "Why is it important to hear the stories of experienced, successful traders?" There are several good reasons.

The first reason is to get an idea of the learning curve involved in becoming a successful trader. Like any other skill, trading requires hours of practice, learning, and hands-on experience—especially learning from mistakes. These interviews are the best way to find the biggest mistakes that even successful traders have made on their way to becoming consistently profitable.

Secondly: experienced, veteran traders have the ability to give you insights and distinctions that you otherwise wouldn't have. People who have been in the trading trenches have the ability to see market events and phenomena well before the average person. This high level of experience and training can be compared to the NBA Hall of Famer. In other words, these people have the absolute highest level of training and years and years of successful playing experience. Think of it this way: if you were learning to play basketball, wouldn't you want Michael Jordan to be your personal coach?

The third reason to learn about successful traders is to give you historical perspective of Wall Street over the last 50 years. This will give you the ultimate perspective.

The goal of this book is to give you new perspectives and wisdom from some of the world's best traders. Let these interviews serve as your personal virtual coach. I am certain that what you read will not only entertain you, but also accelerate your own trading learning curve. I sincerely hope you enjoy reading this book as much as I enjoyed interviewing these traders.

# Eddie Z.

**Matt:** **I'm Matt DeYoung, and I'm here today with Eddie Z., creator of EZBreakouts and COO of EZ Trading Computers. Eddie, I'm honored to interview you today. We've been doing business together for quite a while, and I've learned a lot from you. I hope that, through my interview questions today, people will get to learn some of those same lessons.**

**Today I want to ask you about being a successful trader. Just briefly, tell us how long you've been involved with trading.**

Eddie: My Wall Street experience really dates back to 1987, which is the year I graduated high school. My father was a floor trader on the New York Mercantile Exchange. He traded platinum, natural gas, crude oil, heating oil; all the commodities that were traded on the floor.

Even as a kid, my father used to bring me to the Exchange with him, and I always loved the energy of the place. It was very natural for me, the summer that I graduated high school, to work on the floor before college started. That's really when I started on Wall Street and my interests in the markets really began.

**Matt:** **Thanks for sharing that, because I think it's important for people to know that you've probably seen just about every season of market cycles. You've told me about some successes and failures you've had of your own, which are important lessons.**

**If someone asks you today about the top traits of a successful trader, what would that list look like?**

Eddie: 1. Having a mentor.
2. Getting some form of trading education.
3. Understanding that you need a repeatable method.
4. Having enough capital.
5. Understanding a trader's mentality vs. a

gambler's mentality.

6. Understanding your fight or flight response; paramount to being a successful trader.

Those would be my top six.

**Matt: There may be others that come up as we go, but that's a really good list. One of the things you mentioned for being a successful trader is needing a mentor. What is a good mentor?**

Eddie: People who are successful at anything, if you look throughout history, that they have a coach who's had an incredible degree of success. That's really what a mentor is: someone who's really successful at something you want to do, and then essentially modeling what they do.

A mentor doesn't necessarily have to be someone that you know personally. I have a couple of mentors, and the easiest one for me to model is William O'Neil. He's the creator of the Investor Business Daily and he also wrote a book called *How to Make Money in Stocks*. He was kind enough to put his model into several books. I became so enthralled with the way he looked at the market, and the way he processed the data. For me, it was easy to see his model and then understand all the little intricacies.

The other mentor I'll talk about is my dad. His model's a little different, because he hasn't been easy to systematize or build a model around, but he's given me a tremendous amount in the psychology of trading.

**Matt:** **I want our readers and listeners to take note of a couple things you just said, Eddie.**

**Mentors come in many different forms. I believe I have many mentors that come from books and courses. Another thing I heard you mention about being a successful trader is education. Now, some education is kind of overrated compared to the cost. Some education can be infinitely more valuable.**

Eddie: I do want to mention a couple of things about mentors, first. I think there is one thing you need to be careful about when it comes to mentors: you can have too many. Too many different pieces of information from too many sources... it becomes convoluted.

For example, I find that there are people who really grasp onto one religion. Other people will study multiple religions and grab little pieces of each, but they never really grasp the core of one of them. That can be true of having a mentor. When you get too spread out, it's a mistake.

**Matt:** So Eddie, if I understand you correctly, you need to find someone as a mentor who has achieved the results that you want. That's step one.

Eddie: Definitely.

**Matt:** Then, for step two, you might find people who are easy to model. You mentioned William O'Neil.

Eddie: Right.

**Matt:** Your dad was a little more difficult. After a while, you want to hone in on one mentor; who got the results you want and you really focus on that one.

Eddie: You need to really focus in on their method. Like I was saying, I think people make the mistake of learning a little bit of everything. Maybe that makes sense until you find the one that really resonates with you, but then you do need to go through that process of really focusing.

**Matt:** I made a list this year of the people I like to model most, and it's a very short list. Good advice.

Eddie: I think you can have different models, or different mentors, for different aspects of your life—whether it's spiritual, physical, business, relationships. For example, find a couple in a successful relationship. It's not easy to do.

**Matt:** **Eddie, you are essentially telling people that by finding a good mentor, they become a successful trader. By doing that, they can essentially shortcut the learning curve because they're just trying to model what another person's already done.**

Eddie: Correct. That's a very good summary.

**Matt:** **I think some education is priceless in that way; whereas other education may be irrelevant.**

**As a trader, what type of education is needed to be successful, in your opinion?**

Eddie: It really does go hand-in-hand with having a mentor. You've got to start somewhere, and you have to practice, and you have to have a method. The method really needs to be laid out clearly.

**Matt:** **Just so our readers understand, it's easier than ever to start trading. It's not regulated that you need education, correct?**

Eddie: Marriage is a good example.

**Matt:** **Anybody can become a trader or get married.**

Eddie: That's right.

**Matt:** As a trader, though, what would be the education that someone really needs?

Eddie: In trading, there's so many people who just… they jump in and they're winging it. Why do you need to get an education? You need the basic understanding of the mechanics of how different markets work. You need to understand that there are multiple approaches to trading. You need to understand that you're going to be drawn to certain types of trading. There's a lot of different avenues. Trading is a pretty broad word.

**Matt:** Let's bring it back down to an analogy about flying airplanes. There's a 747 and there's also a Cessna. Those are two really different planes, so the training you'd need is different.

**What would you say is the first step for a good trading education?**

Eddie: To fly any plane, they teach you on a Cessna. That's where you start.

What's the criteria for selecting an education? Find some type of educator or mentor that has a track record of success. That's the first thing. That teacher/mentor needs to teach the markets and the timeframes that you want to trade.

For example, in stocks (which is what I trade), there's day trading, swing trading, and investing. Those all require different types of education.

You have to decide what kind of trader you want to be and then find the right school. Reputation is extremely important. Are there others who've had this education who've experienced success? Are there testimonials?

Unfortunately, trading can lend itself to a get-rich-quick mentality. Any time you have an environment where there's supposed opportunity to get rich quick, you're going to have snake oil salesmen. In the world of trading education, there are a lot of people offering education who have never made any money trading, who have never even traded before. You really do need to be careful and selective of who you pick for education.

That would be the most important criteria, in my opinion: finding a school or a mentor that has a validated reputation.

**Matt: Eddie, you found William O'Neil. In a way, the advice you're giving, you've already followed. Isn't that true?**

Eddie: Yes, and for me, it meant going through a lot of suffering to get to that point. I would not be where I am now if this didn't happen.

When I first started as a stockbroker and trader in the early 90's, all the market did for seven years was go up, and it went up a lot, so trading was really easy. Eight out of 10 stocks worked, so you never really had losers. If you bought a stock, and in three months that stock didn't work, you just sold it and bought something different.

I needed to go through a period of suffering and losses—and losing other people's money as well as my own money—to realize that I had no idea what I was doing. I really didn't have a system or a good mentor. At that time, my only mentor was my father.

My father, through 1997-2000, was on the sidelines because he couldn't believe the market could keep going up. He thought it was going to end ugly. He was very, very early with his call, so he missed the time when the market did, in fact, keep going up. He also missed that parabolic run at the end of 1999.

It was just too many years of the same success; I thought I figured it out on my own. That's probably the absolute worst thing that can happen to an early trader: sustained success. My success was a full seven years of consistent earning. Seven straight years, you start to feel like you're an experienced veteran.

I really got smashed over the head with that crash that happened in 2000. I lost clients, and in some cases lost 70-80% of their account values. I took a substantial personal loss, then realized that I had no clue what I was doing.

**Matt:** **A third thing you're hinting at is a system. What does it mean to have a trading system? What are the core principles that you try to use in your own trading system?**

Eddie: A system is a step-by-step set of rules to locate opportunities and know exactly how to: find them, enter the trade, know when to exit the trade, and know exactly how much of a financial investment or risk you're taking. It's a strategy, a plan.

It doesn't matter where you are in your trading lifetime, you need to have a system that makes sense. My point is that whatever system you invest time in, needs to really resonate with you.

**Matt:** **I want to highlight something. Einstein said that a solution should be the simplest it can be and no simpler, which is a funny thing to say. You're saying to keep it as simple as it possibly can be.**

**How did you get to that point, where your trading system was simple?**

Eddie: If you download any of the trading software platforms that are popular—be it TD Ameritrade, Think or Swim, Trade Monster, or Fidelity—there are hundreds of indicators built into these programs that really don't have a lot of meaning. An indicator is supposed to be a clue about the direction of a stock or a commodity.

The problem is that a lot of these indicators are like a check engine light. It's pretty vague when the check engine light comes on, isn't it? If you've ever owned a BMW, it could mean that you left your gas tank door open. That's all it could mean. 90% of those warnings are worthless.

People download these software programs, they start learning about the different indicators, they start putting them on charts. Suddenly they have charts that have 20 or 30 different indicators and they have no idea what they mean or how they work together, or *if* they work together. That's a big mistake.

Keeping it as simple as possible is definitely a key to success. Every indicator that you use on your trading platform should make sense.

**Matt: The test I would use, is can you explain it to someone else?**

**Eddie:** That's a good test. Is it something you could explain to somebody in under five minutes, and they understand it.

**Matt:** **I have to say, even if you have a mentor, they're going to want you to practice, education's going to require you to practice, and knowing a system's going to require that you practice. Practice takes time, but another thing that trading takes is money.**

**What is the right mindset about how much time, energy and money it will take to be a successful trader?**

**Eddie:** You should only pursue trading if you have a chunk of money that you don't mind losing; losing it won't change your lifestyle whatsoever. You also need to be dedicated to putting in the time.

The main mistake of people getting into trading: they think they're going to be able to trade full-time and make a living, immediately. That equals disaster, putting that level of pressure on yourself. The best mindset is: I have a chunk of money, and if I lost it all it wouldn't change my lifestyle.

I learned this from somebody else: what I would encourage you to do is go to a Gamblers Anonymous meeting to see that that mindset really is a disaster.

**Matt:** **You almost have to feel the pain of gambling in a traditional sense. Listening to other people's stories of the crash and burn, and seeing their emotions, that's a sure way to teach the gambling lesson. I've heard you say that it disappoints you when people label trading as gambling.**

Eddie: I hate it.

**Matt:** **This may be, though, a view that the general public has. On the other hand, some traders may be gambling without even realizing it. What would it look like to view trading as gambling vs. a business?**

Eddie: As a successful trader, I know that genuine trading is not gambling. Having a system, having a methodology, understanding how much you can put at risk on any given day, is not gambling. You *do* need all those things so it's not gambling, and I think for the vast majority of people, they don't put all those pieces in place.

You really do need to see it as a business, and so, what do businesses do? They have revenues and expenses. Revenues means that you can follow a system and it will generate winning trades. Not every trade is going to be a winner; every profitable trader knows that. Part of trading is losing, and those are your expenses. As long as the revenues are more than the expenses, you can make money.

It also means taking calculated expenses. All your expenses should be predetermined; you know how much you can lose. What is your total risk tolerance? I think that's where a lot of newbie traders, and even veteran traders, just can't admit when they're wrong. Maybe that's a gambling mentality, not being able to admit you're wrong.

**Matt:** **You could start a business that, let's say, ships boxes. It sounds like it's not gambling. Isn't it true that, even in business, if you don't have a mentor/education or practice and a system, you could call that gambling?**

Eddie: Starting any business and not trying to find a successful mentor or education is definitely gambling. Just turn on *Shark Tank*. That show is full of people who can't admit they're wrong.

I think being able to admit when you're wrong is one of the most mature things that any adult can do. When was the last time you looked at your significant other and said, "I'm wrong and you're right." For whatever reason, this isn't in most people's programming.

**Matt:** **On the whole, you're successful because there's some small gains, some small losses, and then ultimately some profit.**

Eddie: That's a good way of summarizing it.

**Matt:** **You've talked a lot in your courses about mindset and psychology, and that's a requirement for a successful trader. I've heard you talk a lot about fight or flight. What happens in a trader when there's a fight response vs. a flight response, and how does this impact the profitability of traders?**

Eddie: Fight and flight are actually the same mental state. Let's say you're walking through the woods leisurely, and all of a sudden a big grizzly bear is running towards you at high speed—that feeling of panic is your fight or flight response. That is an actual physiological reaction of the brain, the amygdala telling your body that if you do not run or fight, you will die.

In trading, when you put money at risk, your amygdala gets triggered at different levels. Generally speaking, the more money you start losing, the bigger that bear gets. It's going to trigger that physiological change. Blood flows away from the higher thinking areas of your brain, moving into your muscles and limbs to make you ready to literally physically fight or flee.

A lot of traders will fight; they'll keep trading. The problem is all this blood has flown away from the thinking areas of the brain, and now they can't make good decisions. Another term for it, as a trader, is "revenge trading." You're wrong and you're mad, and you're going to get back at that stock. That's the fight response.

Some traders will never trade again. That's the flight response. The fight or flight response is one single state; what differs is a person's reaction to said state.

This happened to me once. I really needed to step back from trading for a good six months to figure out what happened. I lost over $50,000 in four days. Over the course of a month, it was a lot more than that, and I wasn't going to allow that to ever happen again. There were too many losers in a row; I knew I'd lost something. It was this fight or flight response that had overwhelmed me. It's almost like Dr. Jekyll and Mr. Hyde. You just lose your mind.

**Matt:** **Specifically, what do you do to avoid making rash, bad decisions? Do you have rules?**

Eddie: The most important rule that I have for myself is to not make trading the only thing I do. I have other things I'm working on that are just as important. I'm running a couple of businesses; this slows me down and forces me to wait for the best setups. I don't need to count on my trading to make money.

Then, the other part of it is having a rules-based system that forces you out of the trade when you're wrong. It's as simple as having a stop-loss or a trailing stop; a stop that is ratcheting higher if the stock's moving up. You put it in as soon as you buy the stock. You want to have a stop-loss in. If the stock moves straight down, you're out right away.

It's really just that simple. It's having the net underneath the tightrope.

**Matt: Going back to the list of what it takes to be a successful trader, I've heard you mention that trading's all about trends. When it comes to stocks, there's technicals and fundamentals. These are still all about trends, but how do you view trends and what would a trader need to understand about trends to be successful?**

Eddie: You mentioned three words: trends, fundamentals and technicals. A trend just means a stock or commodity, or some financial instrument where the price is trending up or down over a period of time.

Technicals means looking at a graph of the price history, and deriving all of your information based on that. You're not making any decisions, except on the shape or trend that's showing up on the graph.

Fundamentals is actually taking a look at, in the case of stocks, what companies do, what businesses they're in, and trying to determine if it's a growing or shrinking company.

For me, it's all about the technicals.

**Matt:** **What would a trader need to understand about trends to truly be successful?**

Eddie: The thing to understand about trends, in order to be successful, is that the trend is your friend. The media and your friends are completely irrelevant. All a trend is showing you is pure supply and demand. You need to understand how that supply or demand is being created in that particular security. Whether it's in a stock, mutual funds, hedge funds and pension funds, building big positions in a stock and moving a stock higher, a commodity (like crude oil)... suddenly there's a fracking revolution. You can see that in the price action, or the trend of financial instruments.

All the other stuff is just noise. There's a lot of noise. A lot of people try to pick the end of the trend, and that's where they get hurt.

Being against the trend is not a good idea.

**Matt:** **One thing you mentioned at the top of being a successful trader is having a mentor. I do feel**

that today you've given us a lot of good mentorship. I hope people will read or hear this at face value. Sometimes the best advice sounds simple, but it's hard to master.

What's the last point you want to leave with a trader who is fully and completely committed to becoming successful?

Eddie: I would say don't give up. Let's just say, for example, you're 100% committed to becoming a successful trader, but you really haven't had too much success. Don't give up if you're totally passionate about it, but take some steps back. Take a look at the mistakes you've made and learn from them.

When you come back to it, find a mentor, find some form of education. Take it step-by-step. Don't bet the ranch. When you start trading again, go very, very slowly. It's really about pacing, education and learning from your mistakes.

Matt: I wasn't planning on asking you this, but I have to ask you on behalf of the readers and listeners today. I know you to be someone who's fully and completely committed to becoming a successful trader, and you've gone through it. When you come out on the other side, could you just give us

**some sense of what it feels like to have the lifestyle of a successful trader?**

Eddie: I think it really makes you mature. You learn how to admit you're wrong. The market's going to tell you whether you're right or wrong; listen. I think you learn to be okay with being wrong, and I think you can apply that to other aspects of life.

Do I know every trade's going to work, that I'm always going to make money trading? No; you always have this little part of you that kind of keeps you in check. There's a healthy fear, and then there's the fight or flight fear. There's always a little healthy fear that keeps you in check.

**Matt: In terms of your personal life, has being a successful trader, and all that you've learned from it, given you other opportunities to invest in businesses directly? Do you travel?**

Eddie: Yes. I was a successful trader financially, and because I grew as a person, I was able to start EZ Trading Computers and EZ Breakouts and have fun with those businesses. They became successful, and I feel extremely fortunate to be where I am now.

I think going on vacation is something you have to do to clear your head. Even though I've done well financially, I'm pretty low-key. I had my outrageously over-indulged period in the late 90's. I had to learn for myself, it really doesn't do anything for you. I have an inner peace now. Part of that is learning how to trade. Part of that is learning how to be with my woman. Part of that is just finding a certain level of peace in the success of figuring out things systematically.

I can't overemphasize systems, methods. I think people are looking for instant gratification too much. When it comes to being an expert, there are many research studies that show it takes 10,000 hours of study and practice to really master something. Honestly, trading isn't any different. That might sound like an awful lot of practice, and potentially an awful lot of losses, but you can develop those skills with micro-trading.

**Matt: Eddie, I hope what people hear you saying is how to be centered and enjoy what you do. I hope they hear that it's far easier to go through step-by-step than have 1000 failures. I appreciate your mentorship today, your friendship, everything that we've had together.**

**I want to thank you for the interview and wish you well.**

Eddie: Thank you, Matt, and thanks for your friendship and partnership.

**Eddie's Key Secrets to Remember:**

1. Necessary for becoming a successful trader: having a mentor, getting some form of trading education, understanding that you need a system or a method, having enough capital, understanding a trader's mentality vs. a gambler's mentality, and understanding your flight or fight response.

2. The trend is your friend.

3. The instinct to fight is a bad instinct. Back away.

# Roberto Pedone

Roberto Pedone's fame came when he started blogging a summary of Jim Cramer's *Mad Money*, which eventually led him to contributing content to one of the most visited financial websites on earth: Jim Cramer's TheStreet.com. Roberto considers himself a "Chart Hacker," as his specialty is breaking down charts to find very specific patterns.

**Eddie: I have with me Roberto Pedone, who's currently an outside contributor for TheStreet.com and also runs his own trading website called Zero Sum Trading, which is on Marketfy.**

**First of all, let's talk about when and how you got into trading. When did it all start for you, Roberto?**

Roberto: It all started a little after high school. I didn't work at any brokerage firms and didn't have any mentors that introduced me to trading. I just always had a love for financial markets.

After high school, I did not go to college right away. I dabbled a little into trading first. I was lucky enough to go to college when you could have laptops in classes; I traded every day. I'm sure my business professors were wondering what I was doing. That's how I got started.

**Eddie: What year?**

Roberto: In the 2000s, right after the market crash. I actually got interested as the markets were doing things that were ridiculous. I was seeing stocks go up 50 points in a day. I got interested right after that, which of course was the worst time to get interested in Wall Street and trading. As things moved forward, that's when I got a little more serious.

**Eddie: Was there anything in high school that sparked your interest? Seeing CNBC? Was it a friend of yours who was trading?**

Roberto: I wouldn't say it was CNBC. There were some professors in high school who were into the market. That's when it started, but it didn't really perk my interest until after high school. I couldn't believe what some people were making. Then sure, I was turning on CNBC and seeing stocks do ridiculous things.

**Eddie: You started trading in college. Was there any methodology you were using? What were you basing your trades on?**

Roberto: At first, I knew absolutely nothing about what I was doing.

**Eddie: You're not the first person to say that.**

Roberto: I'm being brutally honest. When I first started trading, I knew absolutely nothing. It was about fundamentals; I would go to a website and read about some company. So when I started out, I tried to find companies that I thought were going to be explosive. I learned really quickly that that doesn't necessarily translate to making money.

**Eddie: It was about the story?**

Roberto: Exactly. I would find some company that perked my interest, and I would literally buy a stock and have no idea where I was buying it. It's funny now, looking back.

**Eddie: I imagine you took some losses in the beginning.**

Roberto: I definitely took some losses.

**Eddie: How did you figure out how to make money?**

Roberto: I think anybody on Wall Street is going to tell you that to learn how to make money, you lose money. That's the best lesson.

**Eddie: I've interviewed quite a few people, and there are some that I've not included in the book because they told me that they never really had a big loser. You don't make the adjustments you need to make until you have that pain.**

Roberto: I absolutely blew up accounts—five figure accounts—which doesn't sound like much now, but when I was a college kid, it was substantial. It's nice to be where I am now, able to help put people on the right track. Hopefully the blow up doesn't happen for them, but it's almost like a rite of passage.

**Eddie: How long did it take you to figure out how to make money? How did you change your way of doing things?**

Roberto: After I blew a few accounts, I couldn't trade anymore because I didn't have the money. My time in Germany as a junior was when I just started to discover technical analysis. I found out from the previous trading experience that if I'm going to base trading on fundamentals—if I'm buying a stock at 10 and I love the story, and then it goes to five, and then it goes to two—does it matter what the story is? I'd just lost, and my draw down was huge. That's when I started digging into technical analysis.

After that, I started back testing systems and discovering patterns that seemed to work with a high probability and some consistency. To be honest with you, now I take technical analysis to the extreme.

**Eddie: Were there any books or teachers referencing technical analysis that you found useful?**

Roberto: Actually, no. People think that's crazy. I stayed away from the books, the websites and everybody else's opinion, because that didn't work before. I'm the type of person that'll get very deep into something once I'm motivated.

At that point, I was determined. I'm going to succeed at trading. After doing surface research on what technical analysis is, how can I discover things? That's really where it went. Today, I'd like to say that I hack charts; that's my philosophy.

**Eddie: Can you define "hack" for me?**

Roberto: A software hacker obviously finds back doors. They're finding different ways of breaking into someone's system. When I see a chart, I want to deconstruct it; I want to hack it. What's the human behavior behind the price action? That's really all it is. Anybody can draw a trend line; that doesn't mean you're going to be successful.

I want to figure out exactly what is going on with that equity. What are the sellers thinking? What are the buyers thinking? Did they try to blow stops out at this level or that level? I apply that mindset to my charts. That's why I call it "hacking," because I'm not doing conventional technical analysis.

If everybody is using conventional technical analysis, people are going to trade in the same way. That's why they will blow a stock through a moving average and then rip it higher after. I say "hack a chart," but it's really just deconstructing the chart, looking at previous patterns, trying to figure out probabilities and where the stock can move next.

**Eddie: Do you have any high probability patterns that you are constantly scanning for? For me, I have four patterns that work.**

Roberto: I have high probability patterns and I will scan hundreds of stocks every night to find those patterns. You have to be willing to dig.

**Eddie: What patterns are they, if you don't mind sharing?**

Roberto: There's a certain type of triangle pattern that I love, especially in small cap stocks.

**Eddie: That's a new one to me. Can you explain?**

Roberto: There are all kinds of symmetrical triangles. The ones that I love, especially in small cap stocks, are when you have a stock in an uptrend. It starts to get into a range that's making higher lows. You draw your trend line up from the higher lows, but it's also making lower highs as it comes off through that base.

**Eddie: Tighter and tighter trading, essentially.**

Roberto: Exactly. What I want in almost every trade is coiled chart patterns.

**Eddie: Tightly coiled spring.**

Roberto: Exactly. I want coiled spring chart patterns, because that's basically sellers and buyers of that equity coming to equilibrium. Someone is going to win the battle when that coil is over. Obviously, if I'm buying something, I'm looking for the buyers to win the battle.

**Eddie: Can you give me a symbol?**

Roberto: Let's take a look at AMRN, a small cap pharmaceutical company. Pull it up on a six-month view, then look at November 2014 right after the 17th, that 1.38 high.

**Eddie: I see it.**

Roberto: If you were to draw trend lines on that chart right now, and then you see how it coils up as we get to January 2015, those trend lines all come together. It comes off the top from 1.38 all the way down, so those are lower highs, basically. You can either draw it from $0.78 up to $0.98, or you could just come across in the $0.90 area. When you draw that pattern from a trend perspective, it completely coils up as we go through January 2015.

**Eddie: It flattens out this very little volume in this very little range.**

Roberto: Exactly. If you look at this pattern in this chart through that whole time period, we had massive volatility leading up to the coil because we went from $0.78 to $1.38. Then you come all the way down to $0.93. That's crazy volatility. I guarantee you most people that traded that equity lost money. As I was referencing, it coils up. That's the equilibrium, that's basically where somebody is giving up in that chart. What I want to see is a stock obviously break out of that triangle.

**Eddie: Does it start to break out of that pattern at $1.20?**

Roberto: You could say $1.15.

**Eddie: Okay, are we talking about the volume picking up around February 5th?**

Roberto: Exactly. The thing I look for in a chart like this is lower lows. If you want another indicator, it broke up through the moving averages at the 20-day and 50-day points. Obviously you know your resistance points there, at 1.13 and 1.20.

I want to try to catch these kinds of moves as early as I can, because I want to get the best price. Obviously they can fail. I always tell new traders that there is no such thing as certainty on Wall Street. There is no guarantee.

**Eddie: Assuming you bought this stock between $1.10-$1.20, how do you gauge where you put your stop order, and if you use one, and how do you gauge a target price?**

Roberto: I do not use stop orders. Mental stops are effective for me. There are a couple of things I look for.

I don't want to see the breakout fail. That would be a huge negative, so if it were to punch up through 1.13 and 1.20, come right back down, and close below those breakout levels, I'm out.

Let's say, hypothetically, I buy that stock early at $1.00. Immediately it does not break out, or it comes back through any of those lows (which would be $0.98, $0.93). You need to get out of it right there because when the pattern coils like that, you don't want to see the stock make a lower low from its previous consolidation period.

**Eddie: On the up side, how do you gauge what a good profit target is for it?**

Roberto: If I knew how high a stock was going to go, right after I bought it, I would be a billionaire. I never know how high a stock is going to go.

**Eddie: How do you decide when it's time to sell?**

Roberto: I try to hold on to as much of that stock as I can, managing my risk, drawing trend lines, watching volume patterns. That's the only way I know how to do it, because I don't know how high it's going to go. I understand risk management and that anything can happen.

**Eddie: You're tremendously focused on the technical analysis, you call yourself a hack, a "chart hack," and there are very specific patterns. Do you teach this?**

Roberto: Yes. I've only been running my service for three or four weeks. I'm sure there are some people using the same types of methodology that I use, who might not take it to the extreme. Maybe there are some people that even take it to a bigger extreme; there's always somebody. Publicly, you're not going to find a whole lot of people who do this. I don't know why that is.

If you look at famous technicians in the market—like Carter Worth, who goes on CNBC all the time —he's never going to pull up a chart and do this kind of analysis. He's going to talk about, like I said, cup and handle patterns. I just gave you the surface view of how I might look at a chart like AMRN, because when I get into my service it goes much deeper. I want to figure out what the behavior on that chart is without trying to develop any bias within that thought process.

All I'm trying to figure out is:

- What are they trying to do with the stock here?

- Who are they trying to shake out of stock?

- Where do I see inflection points?

- Where do I see specific points of when that equity is trading that I think it has a probability of their potential to make a big move?

I'm looking back six months, one year, two years even. Has this stock ever made this exact pattern before and then made a move like this? What's the volume pattern? What are the momentum patterns?

This is what I do at my site. I bring people in, I show them how I do things.

**Eddie: I've come to learn that you're a writer for TheStreet.com and you have this huge Twitter following. Tell us about TheStreet.com. How did you get started with that? It's probably one of the most visited sites on the web for the stock market.**

Roberto: I started a blog and this was when *Mad Money* first came on the air. At the time, I was just trading the markets, and I noticed Jim Cramer moving stocks ridiculously. You have a CEO on, and the stock would spike, especially the small cap stocks. Then he would do his Lightning Round. He was literally moving stocks every single day with his comments.

**Eddie: In real time in the aftermarket, yes.**

Roberto: The moves in the aftermarket would be ridiculous. I thought, someone needs to organize everything he's saying so we can all have it at night. I figured it was a good business opportunity, to be honest with you, because I knew we'd get a lot of traffic to the website.

I started a blog and I tracked everything that he said on his show. I would basically just summarize it. I'd watch the show and summarize it really quickly.

**Eddie: You had a *Mad Money* summary site?**

Roberto: Yes. I don't think I was the first one. I think there was one guy before me, but only by a week or two. What I did was I took it to the more extreme; I might even mention the technicals on it, too. I tried to build it out for traders so they had a resource to see what Jim was talking about. I would be posting this real-time. Even if he went on CNBC during the day and talked about a stock, I would put it on there. It wouldn't even just be for the *Mad Money* show.

Then they started *Fast Money*, not long after *Mad Money*. I started to see the exact same thing.

If Jim mentioned a stock, it would just go off; also known as the "Cramer Effect." Through the traffic on my site, I knew people wanted this information. After that, I was approached by James Altucher. He's very big on Twitter; he used to write for TheStreet.com as well. James had created a site called StockPicker.com.

**Eddie: I've heard of that.**

Roberto: He sold StockPicker.com to TheStreet.com. He asked me to do the recaps for The Street for *Fast*

*Money.* They offered me a really good deal. My writing career blossomed from there because he started asking me to create more content for The Street and Stock Picker.

**Eddie: Cramer's a big fundamental guy and not really about charting. His attitude about charts has change in the last few years, but definitely not about small caps.**

Roberto: That's really why my popularity took off: I asked to write about small caps. I'm sure I introduced an entirely new way to view trading for a lot of traders from a technical viewpoint.

**Eddie: What happened to your blog, then?**

Roberto: I sold my blog. It'd gotten so popular, and then I started to do so much work for The Street. Here I am now, doing my own type of work for The Street, my own research. I got approached by a company to buy my blog, and it turned out to be a penny stock promoter who bought it.

**Eddie: So, what was he doing? He would still summarize but then put a bunch of advertising, promoting penny stocks?**

Roberto: Exactly. They bought it for the traffic.

**Eddie: Trader eyeballs.**

Roberto: You know what it's like when you get these OTC stocks—which by the way, I don't trade any OTC stocks.

**Eddie: Only NASDAQ?**

Roberto: NASDAQ, NYSE, never OTC.

**Eddie: What is your theory there?**

Roberto: There's going to be 1% of companies that come out of OTC that are going to be legit. We all know what they are; they're just promotion machines, all pump and dumps. So much can go wrong in the OTC world. I'm not saying that you can't go wrong with NASDAQ stocks, but I just prefer to stay away from OTC.

**Eddie: I need to mention Timothy Sykes.**

Roberto: I knew you were going to ask me about him. I respect Tim Sykes for the success he's achieved in building his business. I don't like the way he markets himself. I don't like what he trades, even though I know he's been successful with it.

**Eddie: He's usually on the short side, is he not?**

Roberto: He is. If you're going to trade the OTC, that's probably the way to go because he's looking for patterns just like I do. He looks for the patterns in the OTC stocks that have the pump and dump mailer sent out. They spike those stocks and he fades them. I don't know how well that strategy still works because once something gets too popularized, they might try squeezing a lot of those trades.

He actually sent me his book, the hedge fund book, autographed, which I thought was hilarious. This was before he was anybody. This was when I was running my *Mad Money* blog. Obviously, he wanted me to promote his book on a blog.

**Eddie: Moving on, how many contributors to TheStreet.com are there?**

Roberto: There's a lot.

**Eddie: You have a big following. How did the Twitter following start? From TheStreet.com?**

Roberto: When I first started using Twitter, nobody followed me. I guess as my popularity grew through TheStreet.com articles, people really started to notice my technical skills. That's when it translated over to Twitter, because it doesn't take long for someone to read an article on The Street and then Google my name; they immediately find my Twitter then. Eventually, I started promoting my Twitter account in my own articles.

**Eddie: You've had this Twitter following for how long?**

Roberto: As far as a bigger following… I don't have a massive following. I'm closing in right now on 10,000 followers. There are people in the market that have 20,000 or 30,000. Cramer's got something like 700,000. I would say it really exploded the last couple of years during this bull market period. Money is just swimming out there to trade small cap stocks. That, I think, is really what blew it up. As soon as I started to write about under 10 stocks for TheStreet, it just went crazy.

**Eddie: On Twitter, do you have people ask you lots of questions?**

Roberto: Oh yes.

**Eddie: What is the top question you get asked?**

Roberto: "Should I buy this stock?"

**Eddie: People want you to do your own evaluation? They want your opinion?**

Roberto: Yes. I always tell people that if you're asking me what you should do in terms of equity, you've done nothing on it. You haven't done any research. You probably don't even know what a trend line is. I always find it strange that people aren't willing to do their own work.

**Eddie: Right.**

Roberto: I can't give that advice. That's illegal. I'm not a registered broker. People see that I write for The Street and think I can just rattle off advice.

**Eddie: Cramer does it. He does his Lightning Round. For some reason, he has an opinion about every single stock. I don't know how that's possible. He will tell you what you should do with it. Your association at TheStreet.com, maybe that's why people ask you.**

Roberto: I'll write an article about a small cap stock, and let's say it explodes. This just happened a few weeks ago. It was MYMX, this little pharmaceutical company. This stock just went berserk after I put it in an article. I go on the Yahoo message board and I'm seeing everybody say, "What a pit Cramer made." Did you guys even read the article? Did you read who wrote the article?

**Eddie: They just see TheStreet.com.**

Roberto: Yes. People apparently think Jim Cramer writes every article for TheStreet.com. He's apparently writing 700 articles a day and doing all his shows.

**Eddie: What is the top question you wish people would ask you?**

Roberto: I wish people would ask me technical-based questions. I want them to come to me having done some actual work. I think a lot of new traders, they really don't understand the amount of work that goes into this.

**Eddie:** **There's definitely a romance period in the beginning. The worst thing that can happen is making a bunch of money immediately. I was that guy, because I started in the early 90's. Technology was all I wanted to buy, and I was just a stock jock. 80% of those tech stocks worked in a big way.**

**Obviously that doesn't work in reality, but having some success in the beginning can make it feel like it's so easy. I think you must deal with a lot of those people. Of course they want your opinion.**

Roberto: We didn't have all this social media. Now, all these new traders have come up, and like you said, they get some success because they get lucky and just follow the right guy on social media.

When this market eventually comes out of the bull market—and believe me when I say this, it will—this is not going to last forever. All these guys who've had this success by piggy-backing people… it's going to change rapidly.

I'm kind of glad I started my service now. There's a lot of people that have followed me and have had success, and then come over to my service. I can now really get into it with them and explain that it's not always going to be this easy.

You have to have a process. You can't just do something off of what someone says on social media. There is too much going on behind the scenes.

**Eddie: I think you've already answered this, but if you could summarize, what's the biggest mistake you see traders make?**

Roberto: Chasing. If you chase trades, you will blow your account faster than you thought possible. What I see so many new traders doing, and why they end up being unsuccessful very quickly, is they don't have a process. They chase moves, they chase volume when stock hasn't broken out yet.

What happens is, when you do that too many times and those trades end up failing because you weren't prepared, your account bleeds. You might not have the huge loss, but you're going to get stopped out of so many of those trades.

**Eddie: A thousand cuts.**

Roberto: Exactly. Death by a thousand cuts. I'm always emphasizing that you need to hunt trades. You don't have to buy it the first day you find it. Wait for the right setup, let the market show you that setup is going to happen.

I always tell people: develop emotional intelligence. Without emotional intelligence, you're going to be a bad trader. If your emotions are driving your trades, 9 times out of 10, it's going to end up badly.

**Eddie: Emotional intelligence.**

Roberto: Yes.

**Eddie: How do you define that?**

Roberto: People will look at trading and think it's about the money. I'm always telling people you need to stop thinking about the money. Money is a by-product of trading.

When a trader focuses on money, they're not focusing on the process. When you think about the money, that's when emotion becomes involved and you're not going to make the best decision on that trade, which could be to stop out.

I go into every trade thinking that I'm going to lose. I'm on the defense from the get-go.

**Eddie: Do you trade earnings?**

Roberto: Yes.

**Eddie:** **You'll trade in anticipation of an earnings report?**

Roberto: I don't do it a lot. If I do it, I'm only using options in front of my risk. I will never hold equity through an earnings report.

**Eddie:** **One of the oldest forms of social media in the stock market is Yahoo Finance message boards.**

Roberto: The worst.

**Eddie:** **Tell us why.**

Roberto: If there's anyone out there that's listening to this, please don't use those things. The information on those boards... I don't think it could be worse.

**Eddie:** **I don't think it's information.**

Roberto: No, it's not.

**Eddie:** **It's insanity.**

Roberto: It is insanity, absolute insanity. Actually, if you want to go in there and see the kind of mindset you don't want to have as a trader, that's the perfect place to go.

If you want to see emotionally-driven trading at its best, go to the Yahoo message boards.

**Eddie: I've got to think it's even worse on the small cap stocks.**

Roberto: The new thing is StockTwits.com. That's the hybrid Yahoo message board now.

**Eddie: Tell us about your website, which I'm just quickly going to mention is marketfy.com/item/ zero-sum-trading. If you go to Google "Zero Sum Trading," it would probably get you to that page. How do you teach? Is it videos, blogs?**

Roberto: As of right now, what I focus on intensely is the chat room, because I can do so much educating there. I do nightly watch lists where I'm giving people the ideas. I try to go over that with whoever wants to, so they know how to trade those ideas. I'm doing live trades. Have you ever heard of Benzinga.com?

**Eddie: Yes.**

Roberto: Really good website, Benzinga. They launched this Marketfy product so people who want to really see what we're doing, not just what I throw out on Twitter, can get into what we do and what our process is. They launched this so any popular trader can have their own service. JC Parets's a really famous technician; goes on CNBC all the time. He's got a product on there.

They basically host the platform. They take care of all the technology. I can do videos, I have my live chat room, I can send out text alerts. With one click, I can blast everything out to social media, to your email…

**Eddie: Are you in the chat room during the day?**

Roberto: Yes, all day. I'm helping my folks any way I can.

**Eddie: Kind of what you're thinking and doing in stocks. That's great.**

Roberto: Yes. I'm still playing around with a lot of the features. There's just so much in it, to be honest with you. We have a tracking portfolio. They verify every trade we make. If I make a trade, it sends an alert to everybody. I can put notes on that alert and say why I did it, where I want to put my stop, etcetera. You get an alert when I exit the trade as well. I don't want people to just follow trades, I want to teach people why I make a trade.

**Eddie: People want to hear why you make a trade.**

Roberto: Yes they do. To be honest with you, people don't actually want to hear; they just want to follow, but I'm force-feeding what my process is.

I want to build these people up as traders. I want to see every person that subscribes to me become a good trader. I want to see traders have their own process. They can see my process, then they can develop a process that fits their personality and/or strategy.

**Eddie: Do you have books or guides in there?**

Roberto: I do have videos coming. As of right now, I'm doing it more inside the chat room and through blog posts, but it's going to definitely move up to videos. My blog posts are detailed. Everyone is going to know what it is I'm looking at in this trade. Why am I in this trade? What am I looking for? What is the pattern I see? I really go in-depth into how I do it.

**Eddie: Again, the website is marketfy.com/item/zero-sum-trading. Do you have any last words for the readers and listeners?**

Roberto: If you want to be a trader and if you want to be good, you need to be prepared to put a lot of work in. It does not come easy. If you don't have passion, in my opinion, it's going to be difficult to have long-term success. Whatever your process is, even if it's not like mine, you have to work very hard. What is the percentage of traders that fail? I think it's 90%. There's a reason for that.

**Eddie: That's right. I think if you don't have the absolute passion for it and you don't have the drive, it's just a hobby.**

Roberto: Exactly.

**Eddie: Thank you so much for joining me, Roberto.**

**Roberto's Key Secrets to Remember:**

1. The best way to learn how to make money is to lose it... You have to lose before you can win.

2. Technical analysis is everything.

3. The number one mistake that traders make is chasing stock.

# Doc Severson

This interview is with Trading Concepts instructor Doc Severson. Doc's transition from the corporate world, to expert options trader and strategist, is a must-read. Doc's dedicated to understanding which strategies work, and how to hone in the best ones. Doc's got *What It Takes*.

**Eddie: I'm on the line with Doc Severson from Trading Concepts. Doc, it's great to have you. To start off, where does the name "Doc" come from?**

Doc:   Do you remember Johnny Carson of the Tonight Show?

**Eddie: Yes, of course.**

Doc:     He had a band leader, Doc Severinsen. For as long as I can remember, people were mispronouncing my last name and calling me Doc. So, when you combine that with the way that I approach trading, it just makes sense. I've been Doc for as long as I can remember.

**Eddie: The nickname definitely implies intelligence. Tell me, when and how did you get into trading?**

Doc:     This goes back to the mid-90's. I was working in an office of a telecommunications service provider. It was all men around my age, we all traded stocks, in retirement and cash accounts. It just got to be the lingo of the day. If you remember the stock market in the mid-90's, you could stick an empty hook in the pond and come out with something.

I knew then that I wanted to learn how to trade. I remember this discussion very clearly, with a man who told me he basically took a second mortgage on his house so he could buy call options on a stock that he thought was going to explode. I couldn't believe he'd do this.

I'd always taken a very hands-off approach to the market. I remember my very first stock transaction, probably 25 years ago. I walked into an office and everybody was very official. I literally walked out of there, the same day, with a stock certificate. This was how things were done.

As I got into this company and started being around this group, it was all just fun. We were in the communications industry so we sort of knew who the players were and who not to invest in.

I suppose, unconsciously, we were doing our homework. By the time the market topped out in 2000, I had done pretty well. I had done well enough to be able to take small cash accounts and buy a couple of brand new cars. By this time, my 401K was doing very, very well. I could choose to invest shares in my own company instead of going into mutual funds. That's what I did. I had really doubled down at this point, and I ended up getting out right at the top because I left the company and went to somebody else. Of course, I was forced to cash out the shares and roll them into an IRA.

Everything was going great, and then 2000-2002 happened. I had a couple hundred thousand dollars of retirement savings sitting there. I wasn't so silly as to think that there was really any skill behind what I'd done, other than understanding the industry, using limit orders, and understanding how to use margin when I was buying stock. Everything else was trailing stops, but I had never really had any education; I didn't know you could get education. It was just not in the public consciousness.

**Eddie: How did 2000-2002 treat you?**

Doc:    What happened was, I knew subconsciously that I'd gotten lucky. It was very fortunate that somebody got hold of me from one of these enormous brokerage houses that specialize.

A representative came to my house and planted this question on me: "Are you saying that I can't provide value to your account?" I figured they'd gotten me this far, they could take me further. The bottom line is, Eddie, within two years they had divided that account by three.

**Eddie: It went down 67%.**

Doc:    I will take responsibility for some of that because I wanted to be aggressive. With a good fund manager, they should have explained what could easily happen.

In 2003, I was crushed. I wasn't the only person that had gone through this, but I was really disappointed that somebody who'd promised the moon had no clue.

I got a first-hand account of how actual money management occurs. Money management works great in a professional setting as long as the market's heading in one direction. When it changes direction, they don't have any clue what to do.

**Eddie: What happened next?**

Doc: Basically, I stuck my head in the sand from 2002-2004. In 2004, I went to a motivational seminar. At this point, I was just a working slug again. I saw Zig Ziglar do his thing, and I had heard Zig be better.

It was unfortunate to see him like that and it just wasn't motivating.

After a break, I went back into the seminar and all of a sudden someone was talking about the stock market, and that piqued my interest. He proceeded to have me on the edge of my seat, just showing how to do simple option trades.

My wife elbows me. I elbow her back. This is great. Then of course, he puts on his program pitch. I literally leapt out of my seat and ran to the table because I was afraid they were going to sell out. I signed up and I was literally in the classroom two days later, attending a seminar.

I just knew, this is what you're meant to do for the rest of your life. I dove into this stuff with everything I had. I'd get home from work and read about it for three or four hours a night. I ran discussion groups. I would travel to meet with other discussion groups. I signed up for every coaching program that I could buy. I immersed myself. I wanted to make something happen in a hurry.

**Eddie: Who was the teacher?**

Doc:    This was the Investools program at the time, which was a fairly popular program. They took over the mantle from Wade Cook.

They were very good in terms of letting you understand how to use charts to make trades. They were very good at getting you motivated. They were very good at up-selling you into the next program. Probably the best thing I got out of that program was just the personal contact and meeting other people that were really heading in the same direction and forming mastermind groups.

**Eddie: Mastermind groups?**

Doc:    Absolutely. I could not have done what I did without going through mastermind groups because it really does accelerate things.

**Eddie: You started studying options, you became passionate. What happened after that?**

Doc:    I never intended to go into the education business. Obviously, I intended to trade my capital, make money from that, and support my family.

I had turned into the jack of all trades, but the master of none. One thing that's great with options: there's no shortage of strategies that you can learn about. You can learn about butterflies, calendars, broken wing butterflies, iron condors, vertical spreads and bull call spreads. It was my mission to learn every single one of them. I want to be able to reach into my utility box and pull out anything at any given time. You should have seen my account. This is my retirement account too, trading. I was just being very aggressive with it.

What I found was that I was learning how to enter them but I wasn't learning how to be an expert in terms of managing, especially with risk management. I think that's something that comes with more of a sense of professionalism. There was a lot of activity but there was very little progress. There were lots of trades, lots of commissions, lots of experience getting my feet wet with different strategies, but very little forward progress. Of course, when I would take a loss, it was usually wiping out several weeks (if not, months) worth of profits.

Finally, I found a strategy that I was confident was a good fit for me.

My effort at that point was to narrow my focus. I found this strategy called the "Iron Condor," which is a fairly simple strategy. Back then, it was actually a boutique strategy. It really wasn't much in the public consciousness at all. *Are you telling me that as long as the stock trade's within the range for a few weeks, I can make a 10-15% return every month?* All I needed to do was find the right stock.

Fortunately at that time, we had a very mildly trending market. The entry day volatility was actually fairly quiet. Again, through providence of some type, I wandered into this strategy and started trading it in the S&P. I started doing really well with it and all of a sudden was getting a lot of confidence. I started understanding what I was doing.

That was the first lesson I had to learn: to narrow my focus to one trade and one setup. I had gone from doing 30 different strategies to one strategy, being very focused about it.

**Eddie: From the moment that you were at that seminar to the moment when you reached this conclusion, how long was that period?**

Doc:   I was about six months into this, and this is where I learned my second huge lesson. One of the instructors of the class was a very highly respected trader. He just happened to run a newsletter on the side, running this advisory service.

I specifically remember this call. It was for Ryland Homes. It was just a bear income trade, and they made a great case for the fact that Ryland was very likely to stay underneath all-time high prices. We were able to sell a position that was outside of the range that it had ever been before. I liked the fact that it was certainly an outlier. Ryland Homes would have to make all-time new highs for this thing to get into trouble. It had all kinds of different levels of resistance overhead. They made such a great case that I really doubled down.

Again, I'm in my retirement account and I'm using a position. I arbitrarily picked the position size, which is certainly another lesson that I had to learn. What happened was as soon as I entered it, the price started going after the position; challenging the highs. Their advice was not to worry, it was still underneath resistance.

Cut to two days later, it's still coming higher. They still said not to worry about it. Finally, the price breaks into all-time new highs. I'm big-time underwater on this trade. I'm down thousands of dollars. I can't sleep, I can't eat, I'm a nervous wreck. I don't know what to do. I reached out to them one more time. They said I should have gotten out a couple days ago.

Eddie, I was absolutely furious.

I slept on it for a while and I came to the realization that I should be responsible for my own trades. Also, if they haven't figured out how to defend against an attack like this, maybe that's something I should do. This is what really led to my development.

1. Focus on one type of trade.
2. Really understand how to defend a trade so that you know what's going on, whether it's going for you or against you, because so many people get into trades and they don't have any idea.

Those two lessons that I had to go through were probably the strongest things that I've carried from day one: become an expert in one thing, and learn risk management.

The blame game never made anybody any money.

**Eddie: How did that trade turn out?**

Doc: It was awful, but if you think about it in the long-term, it turned out great. If that trade had been a winner…

**Eddie: The lesson wouldn't have been there.**

Doc: Think about how terrible that would have been for my development. That was an expensive trade in terms of tuition, but over the course of my career it's probably the very best trade that I ever made.

**Eddie: I like that perspective. Then you started focusing on the Iron Condors. Then, I guess, you developed some type of defense for if the trade went against you?**

Doc:   This is where I started to branch out, because I really focused in there. Maybe six months later, word had gotten out. I was actually feeding trades to one of the instructors for the Investools Company. I had become such an expert on this one specific trade and how to enter it, how to defend it, how to comprehensively build a trading plan around one stock, that one of the instructors had taken me under their wing.

Doing this for a living was completely by accident. I filled up a vacuum because what I started doing was posting my trades on a blog.

I started getting a following. You know how things go viral without you even really trying for it? Next thing I knew, I had literally hundreds of people following this blog and my trades.

By this time, I was spending an awful lot of time on the road. I was spending a lot of time on the phone. My wife wanted to know when I was going to make money doing this. I found that people were happy to pay for my services, so I started a newsletter. This was about 10 years ago. About a year after I took my first option class, and all of a sudden I was putting out a newsletter. All of a sudden, people have expectations. It forced me to really get my act in gear.

Word got out. Next thing I know, I've got 200 people on board. It just went viral. It's one of those things I couldn't explain because we didn't really have social media back then.

**Eddie: How did you get together with Todd?**

Doc:    I'll never forget that first day, Eddie, that first Monday when I didn't have to show up at my job anymore. It was a real leap of faith.

Thinking back on that, I was really kind of cavalier about it. I would never, never recommend that somebody do it the way that I did, but I had such hunger and faith in myself. I don't think you can put a price on something like that. If you really believe in yourself, there's nothing you can't do.

**Eddie: I totally agree.**

Doc:    I woke up and I had nowhere to go. I had nothing to do. My whole life had been run by these rules about how to conduct yourself.

What I very quickly figured out was if you trade options the right way, you're not that busy. You're not sitting there micromanaging every position, you're just letting it do what it's going to do and you're trading by your rules. Mostly, around then, I was trading monthly positions; I wasn't even doing weeklies. I was better off just leaving it alone.

Investools actually had me out on the road with them. That was fun because it got me out to a lot of cities and I would travel two or three days a week. I would sit in the back of the room and trade the entire day. Again, I think the more people you surround yourself with that are doing the same thing, the better off you are.

To get back to your original question about Todd, I wasn't doing much during the day. That's when one of the instructors asked if I traded futures. He walked me through how to trade the ES.

If you learn about options, it's a minefield of things that you have to understand *not* to do. There are few ways to make money in options and there are thousands of ways to lose. I couldn't believe how easy futures are, but I still didn't know what to do or how to set them up. Actually, I did some research and found Todd. Todd was advertising in the back of a magazine.

What he was offering at that time, and I don't think he still does this, was a full day of coaching. Todd was only three hours away from me, so I was all over that. I got through his program, and two months later I wanted to talk again.

We got along like a house on fire. We talked just about everything but what I came up there to talk about. We talked about running hedge funds and about his experience trading. We also talked about my options because he wanted to understand how to trade options. He actually had an options guy he was working with at that time. He went through a couple of them, but he reached out to me maybe four years ago saying he needed a new options guy.

When you're in this business, most of the time, you're on your own. It's a very isolating business, so to be able to team up with somebody like Todd is great. We can talk about what we see happening in the market, which we do quite often. We can talk about setups, and he's always bugging me to learn options stuff. I've walked him through how to sell cash-secured puts. It's been a good fit. I think we fill each other's gaps.

**Eddie: Options in general are not the easiest concept to grasp. It really takes, I think, some live-trading to get the hang of what they are, how they work, how they trade. I've got to imagine that teaching**

**options is challenging because it seems that it takes a more analytical mind to conceptualize how they work.**

Doc:   That's the one thing that's helped me. I went through the pain and suffering of getting an engineering degree.

**Eddie: You're an engineer, that explains a lot.**

Doc:   All of a sudden, when you put something in terms of some kind of pattern or some kind of function, I'm all over it. Now instead of suffering through, we're talking about making money. It clicked really quickly for me. I'm not saying that's an advantage, though.

**Eddie: How do you transfer that to students?**

Doc:   The other half of what I do is creative.

Call options are just like getting a coupon. You can buy this thing for the next 30 days at this price, but if you wait too long, it expires. What if you were to buy a ticket to the championship game? The face value might be $500. What happens to that face value if the two teams in the championship game end up being Duke and Kentucky? That volatility would go way up. All of a sudden, instead of $500, you're going to be paying $2,000-$3,000.

**Eddie: It makes sense. This Iron Condor position you were talking about earlier, is that still your main weapon of choice?**

Doc:  I would say it's my foundation now because I do things more on a pyramid basis. If you're thinking about building a house, you want to dig a nice, strong footer deep into the soil, down into the bedrock if you have to. You want that foundation for your trading to be solid as a rock.

You need to earn right. You need to build from the ground up. You need those solid, boring, consistent strategies that are making you 5% on a trade. Then, look for opportunities for growth. What you end up finding is that you become more patient because of it. If your only trading activity is some of these hyper-aggressive weeklies or scalping strategies, you're going to be chasing everything that moves and you're going to wonder why your account balance is going down. It's because you're not letting the trade come to you.

**Eddie: Right. So tell us about your options course. Clearly, you're teamed up with Todd. You teach options at TradingConceptsInc.com. Do you have one course, multiple courses? How does that work?**

Doc:  Four years ago we had a flagship program that we called OptionsMD. It's very pyramid-based. It's setting up that foundation and then building on top of it. What I did in this options course is very different. To me, the holy grail of trading—and this is what everybody's after—does not exist as a strategy. The holy grail of trading is when you start to internalize something, when you take ownership and specialize in it. In other words, if you think your success has been accidental, if you didn't earn your success, you will find ways to give it back.

It's not necessarily your typical Trader Psychology 101. People are sick of being lectured. "Be disciplined," but nobody ever shows you how to be disciplined. That's the first problem that I address. People self-identify in the program and say, "That's me." I can teach you that strategy, but the minute it becomes Eddie's strategy instead of Doc's strategy is the minute that you take ownership of it.

People start letting the trade come to them because all of a sudden their subconscious mind is aligned with the goals. Your subconscious mind has been managing you for your entire life. Your subconscious is very conservative; it's trying to keep you safe. That's the very last thing you want when you're putting risk capital on the market. There's a difference between being safe and taking an educated risk with edge in the market, which is what we do.

**Eddie: It does seem like there is an unusually high number of options courses relative to even stock trading and futures trading. It seems like lately, there are more options than anything else. Have you noticed that?**

Doc:    I think there's a reason for that. If you look at the spectrum of trading, you've got stocks, futures, options, forex. Everybody loves stocks, but who can afford stocks today? We've got Google at $550, we've got Priceline at over $1,000. All the moves have already been made, so nobody can afford to buy more than a share or two of their favorite stock. You can't get anywhere on that, so what you're forced to do is dredge through the dogs that are out there—these small stocks that nobody understands. Stocks is a very different and difficult game right now.

What you're finding with futures is that people just don't have the time during the day. I think a lot of opportunity has dried up. Look at the number of seniors that should be retired: they're being forced to continue working.

Very honestly, at 70 years old, people still don't have time to day trade. Forex is still odd. Forex is the place where you're having brokerage accounts dry up and basically cease funds. There's not a whole lot of trust out there. Even though it's a great market—the most liquid market in the world—there's still lack of trust. Where everything comes to a head these days is with options, because you can get the leverage of 10 to 1. Instead of buying the stock for Amazon, you can buy a call option. You can still get the gains of 100 shares a stock for a fraction of the price. That's not the way I trade, but that's what's going through people's heads.

**Eddie: Interesting. So, do you still have that OptionsMD course or do you have multiple courses now?**

Doc:   I've really branched out. OptionsMD is still something that we offer. What I'm doing more of these days is building point solutions. Here's a program for calendar spreads, or here's an Iron Condor introductory program. One of the things that I've kind of come up with over the years is what I call "Fractal Energy Trading." It's just a simplified way of analyzing the market that I see moving today. It's showing me where the edge is.

Then I've got other programs that are tied in with that Fractal Energy Analysis that show simplified opportunities for trading weekly options. What time frame do you want? What's your style? Are you aggressive or searching for income?

**Eddie: In your course, do you teach via live webinar or is it mostly videos?**

Doc:    I decided to shake things up for this version of
        OptionsMD. I created a package program of
        everything that I've ever taught. Then, three times a
        week we're meeting live, and we call this the Inner
        Circle. We started it in February and ended in
        August. I'm not sure if I'll do it again. It's so much
        effort on my behalf that I can't get anything else
        done, but it's really neat.

**Eddie: What do you think is the top question you get
asked by students?**

Doc:    "How do I do this?" Everybody reaches a certain
        amount of competency. Everybody that goes
        through options education learns about options and
        then gets some kind of experience. How do you
        translate that into actual profitability? That's what I
        focus on. If you think about what we've talked
        about in the last hour, just about everything I've
        talked about is essentially how to get over the
        hump, because that's what I help people do.

**Eddie: What would be your number one piece of advice
to somebody who's new to trading?**

Doc:    The two main things that I shared with you earlier.
        Number one: find your one thing. You need to
        figure out who you are and what you do. Get
        experience with a lot of different strategies. Go
        ahead and burn up your "sim" account. Don't spend
        any live money trading until you figure out what's

the one strategy that makes you sure you can do this.

You want get to the point where you're ready to throw open the front door and shout out to the neighborhood, "I'm going to do this." If you're 99% of all traders, you're a jack of all trades and a master of none. You've got to become a master of one.

Once you've decided what trade you're going to master, make it yours. Make it all about you.

**Eddie: If the readers or listeners would like to learn more about what you're doing, what you teach, where's the best place to go to, to learn about you?**

Doc: OptionsMD.com. There's a "Contact Us" form, and my address is listed on the site. I take phone calls, I take emails, or you can just go through the form.

**Eddie: Excellent. I want to thank you for taking the time to do this interview. You definitely gave some great nuggets of advice.**

**Doc's Key Secrets to Remember:**

1. Doc went through the experience of learning many options strategies but realized that to make progress,

he had to start by becoming really good at just one of them. You must focus on one strategy and become an expert at it.

2. There is no one to blame when a trade goes bad. You are 100% responsible for your own results. Don't play the blame game.

3. Once you truly master a single strategy, it will become yours. Instead of forcing trades, you will let the trades come to you.

# Nigel Hawkes

Founder of Hawkeye Traders, Nigel Hawkes began trading in 1986. His only tools: graph paper, a pencil and a calculator. Nigel is now president of one of the most powerful volume trading software systems available today: Hawkeye Traders.

Nigel began his career selling ads for *The Times* and *Sunday Times* newspapers in London. His tireless ambition eventually led him to be a proprietor of a successful publishing company, which he sold for a substantial profit in 1982. Seeking a safe investment, he handed some of the proceeds to one of the world's most eminent brokerage firms.

Nigel then proceeded to follow his passion for sailing, becoming a director of the 1987 America's Cup challenge held in Fremantle, Australia. He was shocked to learn that his broker had lost the capital he'd left with him. This unfortunate event made it obvious to Nigel that it was time to manage his own investments. He began his decades-long journey of research, education and the ups and downs of trading, which eventually gave him the experience to be successful.

**Eddie: Nigel and I have been friends for a couple of years. I think what Nigel does is really special. So, let's just get right into it. The first question I have for you, Nigel, is when and how did you get into trading?**

Nigel: I got into trading by total default. I had a business in England which I sold, and I was invited to be part of the America's Cup team. When I came back, I found that the broker who was running my managed account had virtually lost all the money that I'd left with him.

Because I was single, and I was chipped up after selling my business, I started to look at all the trades that the broker made and thought I could do it. I started to trade myself. This was back in 1986, which was before computers. I did it all on graph paper with pencil and ruler. I studied volume; I really wanted to find out more about volume, so I went to the London Stock Exchange for two weeks, just watching the pit traders. Of course, their primary feel for the market comes from the activity of volume. Pit traders scream when there's activity and when it's quiet they just hang around with their hands in their pockets. That's what I really wanted to follow.

My whole journey in trading really started with a trip to Phoenix. I found the original course notes that Wyckoff came out with when he was doing his volume study, brought them back to England, and my journey into volume as an indicator started.

**Eddie: Traders who stood in the pit, you could literally see which brokers were handling orders for their customers and which ones had buy orders. Do you consider Wyckoff to be your mentor?**

Nigel: He was certainly my starting point, and volume spread analysis, as I called it, was fundamental to his trading. There were three great traders who came out of the late 20's and 30's: Wyckoff, Elliott and Gann, who are survived by their methodologies. Wyckoff is certainly the best and, in fact, there is a university in America that has a Wyckoff course.

The main difference between what I did and what Wyckoff did, was the following:

- In my opinion, data was delayed, so it took time to get across because there were no data funnels. Wyckoff took no account of the open of a bar.

- All the research and work that I have done means the open of a bar is paramount, because it's rather like an auction. When the auctioneer makes an opening bid (say at 100) and there are no bidders, it goes down (to, let's say, 20), and it will likely close out lower (let's say 40 or 60). If he says 100 and it goes down to 80, it will likely go up to 140 or 160.

Today, everybody can see the opening range of a 15-minute or 60-minute bar or daily. That is very important, and that's taken into the Hawkeye volume calculations.

**Eddie: You went down to the London Stock Exchange and started studying. You were drawing price and volume graphs with pencil and paper. Were you using point and figure charts?**

Nigel: No. I was buying the *Financial Times* every morning, and I was particularly trading gold. I just drew a graph of the open high-low close of gold.

**Eddie: How long did it take you to figure out how to make money?**

Nigel:   About seven years, to become what I would call proficient. There was another fundamental building block of my trading that came in during that time. I even reached the stage that if my analysis was saying buy gold, I'd sell it because I was wrong so much.

**Eddie: Your own contrarian indicator.**

Nigel:   Yeah. Then I really started to understand volume. When it came, I was so bruised as a trader mentally that I went through the pretty normal unable-to-pull-the-trigger routine. At this time, Mark Douglas had released his book, *The Disciplined Trader*. He had contact details in his book, and I flew over to Chicago to meet him one-on-one. What he taught me really, really was the final building block and allowed me the strength to trade what I'd been analyzing. He told me to think in probabilities, not right and wrong.

So, I never have a winning or losing trade; I only have a plus or minus trade. If you have a losing trade, you're feeding your subconscious that, hey, I'm a loser too. After I'd done some work on myself mentally, and I'd done thousands of hours in understanding volume, I became successful.

**Eddie: You had quite a learning curve.**

Nigel:   Yes.

**Eddie: I'm going to ask you a couple of tough questions. In those first seven years, did you take any big losses?**

Nigel:  I took one relatively large loss. I'd sold my businesses and I wasn't married at that time, so I had no responsibility. I had a lot of money, so the losses only hurt my pride; they didn't hurt my pocket book.

**Eddie: Okay, but there were more losses than gains over time, I would imagine?**

Nigel:  Yes. Of course, I then also had the other problem that all rookie traders have: they are unable to exploit a trend. They come out of trades too soon, and that's because you can't believe that you're right and it's working.

**Eddie: You think that when traders sell too soon, it's totally psychological?**

Nigel:  Totally.

**Eddie: Interesting. Let's talk about psychology, because it sounds like it was the last building block for you to be successful. For me, it's been the same experience. If you had to name two or three things that are the biggest psychological obstacles to being a successful trader, what would you say they are?**

Nigel: First of all, be abstract from your trading. When it doesn't work out, the odds didn't work out. You're only trading odds when you put a trade on. You've done all your risk analysis. There's always going to be a 15-20% risk on a trade. When it doesn't work out, the probabilities didn't work out. That keeps it abstract from my 'self,' if you like. That has worked very, very well for me.

**Eddie: Okay.**

Nigel: The other one that is very important is to actually have a trading plan. We certainly help people who come to our Hawkeye in developing their own trading plan.

The third thing that I make everybody do is write on an a piece of paper in felt-tip pen: "Do not have an opinion, do not have an opinion, do not have an opinion." So many traders have an opinion on what the market is going to do, where it's going to go to, etc. If you're trading volume, then the volume will tell you. Just trade what you see, not what you think.

**Eddie: Not being emotionally connected to your trades is a really big one. Distancing yourself from the result is so important.**

Nigel: There is a defining moment when you know that you've arrived as a trader. The defining moment, in my opinion, is when you can stop and reverse in a trade. In other words, you've gone long, you're underwater, it's not working; you close the position and go short. You're trading what you're seeing, not what you're thinking. That's a defining moment.

**Eddie: It's really about being in the moment.**

Nigel:  Exactly. Another thing you've got to do is turn off CNBC and Bloomberg.

**Eddie: I tell everybody that.**

Nigel:  When I trade, I trade in silence.

**Eddie: Interesting. So, trade in a zen-like space.**

Nigel:  Exactly. I love that phrase.

**Eddie: A place where your sense of wellbeing is not connected to your trading.**

Nigel:  Exactly. You don't live and die on the last trade. You look at your trades after the end of a quarter, a month, a year… but certainly not day by day. If you're running a shop, you ask at the end of the month how you did, not at the end of each day.

**Eddie: You mentioned volume is obviously your favorite/main indicator.**

Nigel:  Yes.

**Eddie: Are there specific technical setups that you look for? I would imagine you combine volume with price.**

Nigel:   Absolutely. Again, don't take volume in isolation. I always trade volume in triple timeframes. I look at volume on a 30-minute, a 60-minute, a 120-minute. I need to see that there is, on my slowest time frame, no demand volume. On my middle timeframe, I want to see some buying volume; I want some indications of strength. On my entry timeframe, my 30-minute in this example, I want to see buying volume.

Remember, all markets have to go through three phases. They have to go through accumulation, and once markets have been accumulated—this is particularly important for stocks—you go through accumulation, which is fair value. Then the free float of the stock dries up, so it starts to go into uptrend. When it gets into uptrend, it goes into overvalue. Once it gets into overvalue, and then it starts to be sold, distribution takes. Then it returns back down to fair value which is normally higher than the previous fair value. That's why prices zigzag.

**Eddie: How do you determine when you've reached what you call this overvalued area?**

Nigel: Let's use the word "oversold." You will see it in the volume profile on the fastest timeframe and the middle timeframe. You'll see that in the trend run up to that oversold position, that there is continuous buying volume on your three timeframes. As soon as you get to your distribution point of oversold, you'll see that the volume starts to become choppy.

The Hawkeye algorithm will paint red volume, neutral volume, no demand volume. Then you'll see small ranging bars of volume as the buyers are drying up. You'll also see another profile which is isolated highs in an uptrend, isolated lows in a downtrend, and what you would call "island reversals." It's when the middle bar has a higher high and a higher low than the previous and next bar. When you see those, the software paints a yellow dot for you. We're choppy, and distribution is taking place.

Then you'll see the return to fair value as all three timeframes click in with their volume. The slowest timeframe will have either no demand volume (which is white), or selling volume (which is red). The middle timeframe will already have red volume and your fastest timeframe will already have maybe three or four bars of red volume. That's when you know that distribution has taken place.

**Eddie:** You have this software tool and it specifically measures volume. I'm not sure if you're aware, but I have a program called EZBreakouts through which I teach people how to trade stocks. It's very much built on volume and price. Your software tool, does it work on all markets, and what platforms does it work on?

**Nigel:** When we started programming—which only started when Omega Research, which is now TradeStation, brought out Supercharts—I met a colleague in London who had some programming experience, and we taught ourselves Supercharts. That was a major moment. The program was designed for my own personal trading, and then people saw what I was doing and wanted the indicators. I then started selling them. It was never a business that I'd set out to do.

The software is available for TradeStation, Ninja and eSignal. It will be coming in MultiCharts and MetaTrader4.

**Eddie:** You mentioned before that most traders tend to sell too early because they can't believe they're right. Does this tool keep you in trades longer?

**Nigel:** Yes. One of the indicators that comes with it is the trend indicator. We teach people how to have belief in the strength of the trend. We run a free trading room on Wednesdays. Anybody can go to our website and click on the training rooms to see Hawkeye in action. In that, we show exactly the technique that you've asked about.

**Eddie: I, personally, am more of a day trader. How the program paints where the volume is starting to dry up; is it based on transactions on the bid side vs. the ask side?**

Nigel: I'll try to describe the indicator to you, which will answer all those questions. What I do is I look back over a period of 20 bars, and I break it into four groups of five. I look at 20 bars to 15 bars forward to the 15th bar, and I take the standard deviation between the open and close of each bar. I take the standard deviation of the open and highs of standard deviation of the open and the low, and I do the same with the close. I take the close, the standard deviation between the high and the standard deviation between the low. Divide them all into each other, and that is weighted.

I then take 15 to 10 and do exactly the same, but now I'm weighing it against the group from 20 to 15. I do the same between 10 and five, but the last five bars I've taken individually and weighted. I'm getting the DNA, the fingerprint of what is going on with the volumes, and that is because we're doing standard deviation of the range of each bar it calculates. It does over 300 calculations per bar, and that tells me the bias of the buyers and sellers.

**Eddie: What kind of test have you run for accuracy?**

Nigel: Let me start by saying that last year I read an article which said only 4% of hedge funds made a profit, and these people have very sophisticated systems, they have PhDs in math, computer sciences, etc. So with that as a caveat, let me just say that although you can back test in the Hawkeye and you'll get good results, in my belief, trading is a skill set. It's an art form; it's not something black and white. I have seen many, many people over my trading career get hugely excited over programs and algorithms that they've written for trading, only to see them fall on their face six months later.

What works in trend run does not work in congestion. You have to be able to change gears. You have a different technique for driving on snow with snow tires than you do if you're on a flat road in Florida. It is the same with trading.

I have successful traders who make life-changing money. I also have people who use Hawkeye, who just don't get it and can't do it. If you are an anxious person, in my experience, you'll never become a great trader. If you don't do the spadework and learn about Hawkeye and the internals of a market, you won't become a great trader.

**Eddie:** I'll briefly give you an example of what we do and my thought process. I teach something called EZBreakouts. It's for day trading and swing trading individual stocks. It's essentially looking at chart patterns. There's only four chart patterns we look at, but probably the most important one is the cup and handle.

We trade stocks when they breakout and there's a day trading methodology that when they breakout on big volume bars, we buy the stock, and we have a trailing stop that's based on an exponential moving average. That isn't really tremendously different from what your indicator is, but my question is, how can I incorporate your trade management tool, your volume tool, into what I'm already doing? Would I get better results?

**Nigel:** You'll get far better results because what you're doing is trading blindly. You've got to remember a lot of other traders are already looking at the same things. A lot of people trade pattern recognition breakouts. You need to know that there's enough volume brewing there to be able to push it up.

That is why I believe that a lot of educators teach people to buy the first pullback. Price breaks out, everybody in the world sees the moving average crossover or the cup handle being broken, and they jump on board. There's not enough attendant volume; it goes up, comes back down, tests itself and then goes. That is where volume will save you, because if it's a false breakout there won't be the volumes coming in to show you. When it comes back and tests itself, that test is validated, or that breakout is validated because there is sufficient volume.

**Eddie: Moving on, do you have any favorite markets that you trade?**

Nigel: Trending markets.

**Eddie: You'll trade anything as long as it's on trend?**

Nigel: Anything. A lot of people have what I call "data overload." They have far too much coming in, far too much noise on all their screens. A lot of trader computer screens I see… I'm horrified. They look like graphic artists, not traders. How their brain can assimilate all that information is an impossibility.

I think you've got to start slowly and build up the patterns you're looking for. I look at my triple timeframes and scroll through the markets. I particularly trade longer-term because I've reached that point in my career that I don't want to be staring at a computer all day. I particularly like the commodity markets, the currency futures and Forex. That's why one of my indicators I call "roadkill." I don't want to fly out all over the desert and forests, trying to kill something. I'm a lazy guy; I just want to see roadkill.

And then, Eddie, the most important thing that people don't teach is how to trade the trade. When do you exit? Everybody talks about entries; very few people talk about exits.

Then how do you capitalize on a trend run? We have something called the Profit Accelerator. Again, it's based around volume, and this is telling you when to add to your positions. We did a lot of work in the early days; I added to positions and came up with a formula which was 1-3-2-1. So if you took, let's say, 100 shares and add until you're up to 700, then get out of them all at the same time. You've got to leverage into these trends. Trends only exist for 30% of the time; markets congest for 70%. When they do come along, don't spin the coin evenly; you've got to trade them aggressively.

**Eddie: 1-3-2-1. Since about 2007, just about everything went electronic. In 2004, I know at least on the New York Mercantile Exchange, it was still 90% pit-traded. By 2008, it completely reversed. How do you think that's affected the markets and how do you think that's affected your indicators?**

Nigel:  Our indicators became better. If you remember, the markets held back volume. When it was the pit traders, they put estimated volume out and then gave the real volume 24 hours later. Today, you get real volume immediately. The analysis became more robust because you didn't get estimated volume.

**Eddie: Okay, let's move on. Hawkeye Traders, not only do you sell indicators, you teach. You have trading rooms, and as you mentioned, you just got done with your own conference.**

Nigel:  We do them in America twice a year. Once in Santa Ana, south of Los Angeles, and once in West Palm Beach. I'm doing one in Singapore at the end of May, and we've got one in London at the end of June. Occasionally I do one in Australia.

**Eddie: As an instructor, what is the top question that people ask you?**

Nigel:  I think it's what I said virtually right at the beginning. How can I stay in a trade? What gives me the belief that this trend is established and how do I stay in it?

**Eddie: Okay. My students, the top question I get asked is can I make a living doing this?**

Nigel:  I took that as an obvious question. I was thinking more on the technical side. Of course, the main question is, is this feasible? The answer to that is yes, it is feasible, but not straight away. You've got to become consistent in your trading, even if you're running a demo account. In my opinion, you can't trade out of the box. You need to put in that mental strength pillar.

I'd like to say that the biggest decision as a trader you will ever make is the timeframe you trade. Nearly everybody I see fail at trading is trading the incorrect timeframe for their personality. I just find it baffling that people start off trying to scalp the S&P. The S&P is the most sophisticated market in the world.

Make your money by doing micro lots on slow markets, and then when your pot builds and your skill set grows, go into the fast markets.

**Eddie: Absolutely. Select a timeframe that fits your personality. What's the fastest timeframe that you think is acceptable?**

Nigel: For somebody who's just started to trade?

**Eddie: Even someone who's sophisticated. I consider myself a day trader and I trade off of a 5-minute chart. I only trade stocks, and I'm looking for volume as well, institutional accumulation. Do you think that's too fast?**

Nigel: Probably. You see, what we're doing is we're taking random data, price data. When you select a timeframe, you're taking random price data and then smoothing it into a timeframe where you have a high and a low. Then you are doubly, triply smoothing that timeframe by putting whatever indicators you wish on it. It's all about the vibration of the market.

**Eddie: Do you believe in day trading?**

Nigel: Yes, but I think it should only be part of your overall portfolio. I would like to see a minimum of 50% position trading.

**Eddie: How do you define position trading?**

Nigel: Daily/weekly.

**Eddie: It's grabbing a position while the trend is taking effect and then exiting when the trend is over, as indicated with the volume?**

Nigel: Also, use the price accelerator. I'd much rather trade the trade or trade the trend rather than have to find a new trend every time. Once something is moving—as we talk today, the US dollar is on a belter of a trend—just looking at that and figuring out what's happened. The money you could have made out of the euro USD trade is huge, as most other currencies against the dollar.

**Eddie:** **Obviously we had a big sell off in oil, which seems to have found at least a temporary level. Is that down trend still intact, do you think?**

Nigel: Yes.

**Eddie:** **Okay, so would you call this just a lower fair value area?**

Nigel: I'd call it a congestion area in a downtrend. Whether it becomes accumulation in this down area, I want to see what happens on the weekly chart. Funnily enough, we went over this oil chart in detail in the seminar I just held. At the moment, there's been no sign that the testing volume has been proven. I see no strength coming through on the weekly and certainly nothing coming through on the bi-weekly or monthly. I think this is a bit of froth at the moment. It might develop, but I'm not hedging my bets.

**Eddie:** **Let's say oil is around $49. If you didn't have a position in oil right now, would you say it's an opportunity to short? Is there a specific support level you want to see it come through before you would short it?**

Nigel: I'd want to see it come out of this sideways movement, and the volume profile start to change so that it actually breaks down underneath. Markets will always test themselves. I want to see the weakest point, around 49.25, 49.50. Then I want to see some high volume come into that, which would give it the momentum for the jackhammer to go through to the next phase and go down.

**Eddie: How long do you think it would take for you to see that volume? Would you need a several timeframe confirmation of that volume?**

Nigel: No. If it goes through those price levels on high volume and then comes back up on low volume, I've got it.

**Eddie: You wouldn't be shorting the initial breakdown, you would wait for the bounce up?**

Nigel: My volume algorithm will show all that. We're going through on some high volume. I want to see where the close of the bar is that has gone through it, and it won't automatically just go short then. It would look for the profile I've just described and then go, because we'll be looking at the weekly to see what the accumulation volume of that week has been and whether that is confirming the faster timeframe. You don't trade one timeframe in isolation when you're trading volume.

**Eddie: Does the algorithm actually send the orders?**

Nigel: No.

**Eddie: It just has the indicator and the paint bar?**

Nigel: Yes, it's got the indicator; you can have it as an indicator or as a paint bar. It has a trend module on it. It has a heat map showing you various trends clicking in and out. As I said, anybody who wants to see this can go into the free room that we run every Wednesday where my partner Randy Lindsey, who is a very competent trader, shows the whole Hawkeye suite.

**Eddie: Great. So tell me, what do you think is the number one mistake rookie traders, and even veteran traders, make?**

Nigel: The rookie trader is undercapitalized and overtraded. That would be what the rookie trader's main mistake is. When I say undercapitalized, I mean they're undercapitalized for the incredibly fast timeframes they're going into.

The professional trader, I would say, becomes too set in his ways and a little arrogant. Particularly, I've had a lot of expert traders come to Hawkeye, and when I work with them, their main problem is patience. They jump over everything too quickly because that's what you had to do in the pit. Being a home trader, you can sit there and see the setups, and that's why if you wait for the setups, on the right timeframes, I believe you can be hugely successful.

**Eddie: I think you've answered this question already, but your personal greatest strength in trading is your ability to be abstract and disconnected?**

Nigel:  Correct. I don't live and die by my next trade. Trading is a business, and as long as you've got customers coming through the door, you don't close the business. As long as you've got plus trades coming in, you don't close the business.

**Eddie: Tell me, what would be your number one piece of advice to a trader who's just taken a huge loss?**

Nigel:  Go for a walk. I would tell them to analyze what they did. I would ask them to go to their trading plan and to their money management and see why that was allowed. You'll probably find that they had an opinion, and they overrode the opinion that was telling them to get out. I believe that you should exit the markets not on a stop, but on understanding when the volume is coming in against the trend, or another indicator is showing you termination of the trend. Most people put stops too close to the market.

So, it's a money management stop, not a trading stop. A stop is there if it goes all wrong and I'm fast asleep in bed. If I'm not 100% sure, I'll take 50% off on the position.

**Eddie: A stop is like catastrophic loss insurance. It's the disaster plan.**

Nigel: Exactly.

**Eddie: You want to sell when your indicators tell you the accumulation volume is changing. The volume patterns are changing.**

Nigel: Absolutely. Ignoring your trading plan is basically gambling, not trading.

**Eddie: As somebody who's been trading for 20 years and teaches trading, I often hear that trading is just gambling. Of course, you and I know that's absolutely not true, but a lot of people believe that.**

Nigel: I think there's some strength in saying that it is similar to gambling, and I think that it isn't true when you're doing longer-term stuff. The faster the timeframe, the less robust any system becomes.

There is a difference between gambling and trading. In gambling, you have a finite win and a finite loss in a finite time period. In trading, you have unlimited risk, unlimited gain, and you choose the timeframe. That is the main difference. Also, of course, it is a business.

**Eddie: What would be the defining things that separate trading and gambling? Firstly, timeframe, and secondly, having a trading plan?**

Nigel: Understanding market structure takes you away from gambling. When you sit at a roulette table or a blackjack table, there's no structure. There's little structure in gambling, whereas in trading, there's huge structure.

There's a friend of mine in England who's made a fortune out of horse race gambling, but he's structured. He discovered right at the beginning that there was a correlation between the people who write in the newspapers and tipsters on horse races, and the stables where these horses are trained.

So, he wrote a computer program that went out, he got all the back issues of *Sporting Life*, went through all the major tipsters and found the correlation between certain racing yards, stables and certain tipsters and horses that had been held back. I've got to tell you, when I go to visit him… I get lost going up his driveway, he's made so much money.

**Eddie: Is that because horse racing was manipulated?**

Nigel: Yes.

**Eddie: When you talk about structure in the markets, can you be specific?**

Nigel: Yes. That is why I'm a firm believer that you need to have triple timeframe. You want to see what the slow market is doing to the mid-market to the fast market. That is what I call the market structure. Markets are very fundamental in their structure. As I said earlier, they go through the phase of accumulation, price move, distribution, return to fair value and zigzag.

When you can see that the market structure on a weekly is in place—and when I say in place, you can see that accumulation volume has gone through in the bottom of a downtrend and you can see the price bars getting smaller in range—you know that you have market structure coming in for termination of that downtrend and accumulation has taken place. You then go into your daily and can see that on your daily, you've got exactly the same profile but you can see the prices have been accumulated on the daily and they are starting to move up on wider range bars. Then you might drill down from your daily to a 720-minute if you're trading Forex or a 360-minute or even a 30-minute, and you can see that that, yes, is now in a belter of a trend.

**Eddie: In conclusion, first of all, I really want to thank you. I'm very interested in what you do, and I definitely am going to take a look at your volume indicator. Is there anything you'd like to talk about in regards to Hawkeye Traders in conclusion?**

Nigel: Thank you very much for the interview today. I've enjoyed it also. The point that I'd like to make in conclusion is that I've been on the other side. We as a company, we're small. We have some other traders who join us running trading rooms and I really, really ensure that we are as ethical as we possibly can be. We don't try to just take money off people; we want them to be successful. I don't run any advertisements, I rarely go to traders expos and speak. The finest form of advertising is recommendation from existing users, and that's where our business comes from.

Hawkeye Traders has been around since 1996. I should be far, far larger in this business than I am, but our marketing is absolutely terrible. We should be a lot better, but if you come to HawkeyeTraders.com, have a look at our suite of indicators. Look at the videos. I try to be a one-stop, so I have that relationship with Dr. Kenneth Reed for the mindset to give you the strength. I have the indicator packages, and we have the education. It gives you what you need to become a successful trader.

**Eddie: Very good. Again, thanks Nigel.**

**Nigel's Key Secrets to Remember:**

1.  When it doesn't work out, don't blame yourself. The probabilities just didn't work out. Nurture your self-worth as a trader.

2.  What works in a trend run does not work in congestion. Trends only exist for 30% of the time; markets congest for 70%.

3.  Trade anything that's trending.

# Todd Mitchell

Todd Mitchell, founder, CEO, and head trader of Trading Concepts, is truly an inspiration to thousands of people, redefining possibilities and opening doors of opportunity for Trading Concepts students.

For Todd, trading isn't just a career or a business, it's a lifestyle and a passion. He's been at it for 30 years, dabbling in many markets over the years, building his experience and skills, and mastering the parallels that make certain techniques work no matter what market you trade. As Todd says, "A chart is a chart, regardless of the financial instrument."

**Eddie: I'm on the line now with Todd Mitchell from Trading Concepts. Todd, it's great to have you.**

**The first question I have for you is where did trading begin for you? When and how did you get into trading and when did it all start?**

Todd:  It all started back in 1985. My father was trading and he was just a small retail trader. He owned his own business and would trade mutual funds. He got into trading the S&P 500 futures when they were introduced. I started updating his charts on an art table. I took the *Wall Street Journal* every day, took the open, high, low and close and plotted the daily bar charts for the S&P, pork bellies, T-bond futures. That's how I got introduced, and I just took to it. My father was reading books and he would give them to me and I would ask him a bunch of questions. It was probably when I was a sophomore in high school that I started actually learning. I put my first trade on in the spring of 1988 after a couple years of charting the markets and learning all about them.

**Eddie: Do you remember your first trade?**

Todd:  Actually, I do. I believe it was early May 1988 in the t-bond futures. I remember I made like $246.

**Eddie: Awesome. At least it was a winner.**

Todd:  Yes, it was a winner. Then, the second trade was an S&P trade. Really, for the first 5-8 years, it was nothing but the 30-year t-bonds and the S&P 500 futures contract.

**Eddie: Back then, how did you place the trades? I imagine you had to call a broker who would call down to the floor.**

Todd:   Oh, yeah. It was Lynn Waldock.

**Eddie: Lynn Waldock, sure.**

Todd:   Yeah, and I had to place those orders through the phone. I think a round turn trip at that time was about $23. A little more expensive than today, but the S&P 500 at that time was $500 a point.

**Eddie: When you called in, how long did it take for you to get an execution or a fill? Do you remember?**

Todd:   It was probably a solid minute or so.

**Eddie: Yeah.**

Todd:   After a couple years, I actually was able to dial right to the floor.

**Eddie: Okay.**

Todd:   They bypassed that middleman and I went right into the floor. It was quicker at that point, but it's so much slower than pushing a button.

**Eddie: Right, right.**

Todd:   Much different.

**Eddie: So, how long did it take you to really figure out how to make money?**

Todd:   It probably took me 2-3 years. When I first started, I started with, I think, $16,000. In the first two or three months, I think I dropped to $10,000. My father felt bad for me. He was like, "Do you want me to just give you that $6,000 back and you can stop trading?" I was like, "No. I know I can get it back and I know I can make a lot more." Within the course of the next six or seven months with that persistence and the discipline, I took that $10,000 and took it up to $37,000.

At that time, I was trading in my college dorm room. I had charts on the walls. I was plotting open, high, low and close, and doing my own analysis. So that's how it all began. I just thought trading was very stimulating.

**Eddie: Interesting. So when you first started, was there any system or methodology that you were attracted to?**

Todd:   I was using a couple variations of a system that Larry Williams was teaching at the time. It was really based on some of his philosophies. It wasn't like day trading today, where you would watch the live data during the day. I was in one day and I was out the next day, unless I got stopped out with a loss the day of entry. That's how I started.

**Eddie: Was he your mentor?**

Todd:  My mentor really was my father, because he got me into it and showed me a lot. He had bought a couple of methods from Larry Williams, so we were using those. He was just a part of the puzzle at the very beginning and gave me a little bit more concrete, objective rules. Would I call him a mentor? No; I've never talked to him. Like I said, I used a variation of a couple of his systems at the time.

**Eddie: Right.**

Todd:  I would say my father was my mentor. He really taught me a lot.

**Eddie: Is he still trading?**

Todd:  Oh, he's still very active.

**Eddie: So, when you finished college, did you go right into Wall Street or did you take a regular job?**

Todd:  Actually, I started trading. I graduated in December of 1990. Knock on wood, I've never had a real job. I've always been able to trade, so it's been 25 years now.

**Eddie: Wow.**

Todd:   I'm fortunate and blessed because trading is just phenomenal. It gives you the flexibility to come and go as you please, although I'm addicted and I'm here all day. With the family, we travel, we do things, and trading does give me that flexibility.

**Eddie: Right, right. What markets have you traded in the past, and what markets are your main focus right now?**

Todd:   Basically, I would say from when I started up to 8 years ago, it was the S&P 500 and the E-mini futures. So, it's really always been the S&Ps, the bonds, and obviously the E-minis since they started trading. I would say that's been my main bread and butter for the day trading.

The last 10 years, what I've done is I've been able to take the principles that I use on an intra-day basis and basically apply it to all markets; ETFs, stocks, even the forex. I trade all those markets very actively, so I do day trade still but I very actively swing trade as well.

**Eddie: Okay.**

Todd:   I have 20 or 30 positions at a time. Again, the swing trades last anywhere from one to seven days, I would say.

**Eddie: Did you say 20 or 30 positions at a time?**

Todd:   Yeah. I mean, last Friday on the open, I exited 15 trades right there within five minutes of the open.

**Eddie: Wow. How do you manage that many? Doesn't it get hard to manage mentally?**

Todd:   If you've got a method that's 95% objective and you've got the rules in place, then it's a matter of being automatic in your process, and that's the way you've got to be. I mean, when you day trade, I like to call it the 80/20: 80% should be pretty mechanical and methodical; you've got to have a process. The other 20%, there is discretion. To make day trading—especially the futures—100% automatic without any human intervention or thought, I think that's wrong. You've got to have discretion. I've been trading for so long and the S&Ps have always been my main bread and butter, that after that many years of watching the market day in and day out, you do get that feel.

**Eddie: Right.**

Todd:   For the day trading, there is discretion. When I'm day trading, how many positions do I have on? One. The swing trading is a different story. I believe when you swing trade, you can make swing trading more mechanical than actual day trading. Everyone's got their opinions, but this is the way I do it.

I can have 15 or 20 positions on and I'm really not doing much during the day other than putting the trades on, having my limit waiting for the market to hit them. I'm either executed or I'm not in the trade. Then, I'm not really managing the trade until the next day. Whenever I enter a position, I've always got that stop in place. At the end of the day, I move my stops and/or look to take profits the next day. Does that make sense, Eddie?

**Eddie:** **Yes, but we probably need a little context before that. For me, I trade a lot of cup and handle chart formations. You're probably aware of William O'Neil, the founder of the Investor Business Daily, he's got a system called CAN SLIM. For me, it's more about his chart patterns than it is the fundamentals, because the chart patterns, in my opinion, just tell the whole story. I'm curious, for you, is there a set of chart patterns that you absolutely love? What are your guiding principles? What would force you to enter a trade?**

Todd: My guiding principle when trading stocks is that I'm looking to buy pullbacks and relatively strong trends. Of course, you can flip that around. If the market is trading down and you're in a defined down trend, then I'll be looking to sell pullbacks. I'm a big pullback trader. You can define the pullbacks in terms of some type of support zone using Fibonacci retracements, maybe some moving averages. I also trade complete, objective, mean reversion algorithms.

**Eddie: Mean reversion, yes.**

Todd: You know what mean reversion is, right?

**Eddie: I know what it means, but if you had to explain it in three to five sentences, what does it mean?**

Todd: I've got six rules that I can literally scan the market with and I will pullback the stocks or ETFs that are setting up. Once I get those setups, once I have a very short-term, extreme oversold reading, I will look to enter the next day on a pullback even further from where that scan brought me to. Those stocks or ETFs, I'll get back on maybe 1% or 2% intraday pullback from the already existing extreme short-term oversold condition, if that makes sense. So, it's time and price. It's got to come down pretty quick and it's got to be in the defined uptrend. I like three, four, five, consecutive lower highs and lower lows in a defined uptrend.

**Eddie: I see.**

Todd: Like one of the simple patterns. I like to try to keep it as simple as possible.

**Eddie: Right.**

Todd: Does that make sense? I hope I'm not too vague.

**Eddie: It sounds like, to me, you're looking for stocks or markets that are in a strong, longer-term uptrend. When they tend to get overbought, you wait for a pullback and you have a way of defining what that pullback looks like before you enter.**

Todd: Exactly. I would only trade stocks or ETFs with over, let's say a half a million or a million in volume, in the last 21 days. It's got to be trading over at least $10 a share. You've got to have a historical volatility of at least 25, so it's got to be a mover. I like to use a two or three bar RSI so that when you dip below five, that's one of the setups, and then looking for a larger, intraday pullback using a limit order. Those trades last anywhere from one to five days.

**Eddie: Is this the same stuff that you teach?**

Todd: Yes, it's a variation of what I teach. I teach a lot of different methods which depend on markets. I have certain setups for trading stocks and ETFs. Then of course, the same principles apply for day trading the E-minis, but it is a little different.

**Eddie: Right.**

Todd: The guiding principles are very similar.

**Eddie: Okay. Would you consider yourself a pure technical trader? You never look at the fundamentals of a stock?**

Todd:   I never look at the fundamentals, actually.

**Eddie: I don't either. To me, it's just a story. In my opinion, all the story is in the price and the volume, and if institutions are accumulating it or not.**

Todd:   Exactly. Everything is represented in a price chart. I'm all about charting. 99% of the time, I don't even know the name of the stock, just a symbol.

**Eddie: Right. So, what's the biggest loss you ever took?**

Todd:   I've never gotten killed on any single trade, because at the very beginning, I learned some hard lessons from friends who didn't use stops, so I always use a stop. Position sizing is very important.

I learned very early on that when you take a trade, it's got to be no more than 2% of your entire portfolio. A $100,000 account should never risk more than $2,000 per trade. I actually think that's still high. I think 0.5% to a little over 1% on any single trade should be the absolute most you should risk. I would say I've never, ever lost more than 2% on any single trade thanks to keeping stops. It's pretty simple not to get killed.

**Eddie: You have no history of suffering with trading?**

Todd:   There's the pain of going through several consecutive losing trades, but on any single trade, no, I've never had a catastrophe. Again, I learned early on of the importance of stops. My older brother's good friend, who worked for my father, took me under his wing.

One story I do have happened in October of 1989 in that mini crash; the S&Ps that day hit a high of 262. I remember I was in my dorm room and I was very tempted to go short the market, but I didn't. My brother's friend was long coming into the day, and he was up about ten or twelve points on four S&P contracts. This would've been $500 a point back then.

**Eddie: Right. The full-sized contract.**

Todd:   Right. That was a pretty nice position. He was up $12,000 or $15,000. He left the office that afternoon at about 2:45PM.

At that time, it was Financial News Network (FNN) that was dominant. He got home, turned on the FNN, and the market had moved from 262 to about 228; almost a 40-point intraday drop, which at that time was huge. He not only lost what he was up— $15,000—but he lost about $25,000 more.

I saw that firsthand, and that took him out of the market. To my knowledge, he still doesn't trade to this day. That early lesson, only about a year into my trading, really scared me.

**Eddie: Yeah, that's great. That was the story I was looking for. Everybody has to have at least one of those stories.**

Todd: Exactly. I know it's hard to believe that I've never had a story like that personally, but it's just because of that incident; it taught me to be smart. I was very adamant about using stops, and I'm still using them today.

**Eddie: I hope that in your courses, you reiterate that. Having been a stockbroker for so many years, I know a lot of people just don't get it. I think that's why 85-90% fail. Their need to be right totally exceeds having smart risk parameters (such as stops).**

Todd: You're correct. Trading is pretty counterintuitive. You're not trained to think the way we need to think to be traders. In school, to get an A or a B, you can't get many wrong. People don't want to be wrong. Trading is about making money, not necessarily about being right.

**Eddie: Exactly. Tell me about what you teach. Tell me about trading concepts.**

Todd: Trading concepts, for me, happened by accident. I was a full-time trader. The only seminar I've ever been to was in 1991. I don't know if you've ever heard of Kent Calhoun?

**Eddie: Yes.**

Todd: He was big into price action, so I went to his seminar. I met someone who knew Kent personally, they gave me his number, so when I got home I called him. I went over to his house and he was trading. I spent some time with him and realized he didn't know what he was doing.

He was charging clients astronomical amounts of money; $3000-$5000 to spend two days with him. After I spent two weeks with him, I knew he was consistently losing money. I thought he was doing a disservice to the industry. That's what gave me my drive. I put an ad in Stocks and Commodities back in August of 1994. I trained my first clients in early December of 1994, and that's how it all began.

I've never looked back. It's been a little over 20 years now. We've got programs for day traders, for forex traders, I've got Doc Severson. He's my main options guy. He's got some great educational products. He's a great trader himself. Actually, he became a student of mine back in 2005.

Everybody that works at Trading Concepts has been a student of mine at one time. I'm always looking for talent within, people that understand what I'm doing and have learned from me. I think it just adds value.

**Eddie: What is your most popular course?**

Todd:   We've got a lot of different programs. My flagship product, by far, is what I call the "E-mini Success Formula 2.0." It's everything that I do on a daily basis; everything is in that program, 27 modules. It's a building block.

**Eddie: Now, do you teach that live or do you have a set of videos? What does that program look like?**

Todd:   Each module has a PDF and a video, anywhere from 20 minutes to an hour long. I've got my trader business plan in there. Then I've got a member's area where you can see a chart with all my trades and the reasons behind the trades. Then I take it a step further by putting together a video.

**Eddie: That's what you were doing this morning?**

Todd:   Yes. I do daily blogs too. I would say probably 80% of the time, I record my live trades and walk people through them. There are about 13 years of videos that are archived in the member's area.

**Eddie: With forex, the volumes are not necessarily accurate. How do you account for that?**

Todd:   It's about the chart patterns; I do not use intraday charts for the forex, I use the daily bars. My smallest timeframe is a 240-minute chart. Those trades are just swing trades based on the same patterns and the same principles that I teach in the E-mini program.

Doc and I came together and we created a stock trading program as well. That's using all the patterns and the formations that I use for the day trading. There's a lot of options and strategies in that program. Doc's got some really popular programs. Options are a hot deal with the weekly options, so he's got a bunch of weekly and monthly programs.

I don't know if there's a most popular program; everyone's needs are different.

**Eddie: Clearly, you're a teacher. What question do you hear most from students?**

Todd:   One of the questions I hear often is, "If you're so good, why do you even bother teaching?" That's a big question. I love answering that, because quite frankly, teaching still does not take me away from trading. I'm definitely more of an extrovert than an introvert. If I wasn't teaching, I would have no outlet.

**Eddie: Trading is pretty lonely.**

Todd:   It is a very lonely business, and I'm very much an extrovert. I love talking to people, teaching people. It doesn't take me away from trading so I've got the best of both worlds.

I learned very early on that teaching makes you better because you're constantly reinforcing what you're doing. You've got people looking over your shoulder, so you're more accountable. I'm on my game, people are listening to me. They're seeing my every move, and so I can't get lackadaisical.

**Eddie: You've got to practice what you preach. You've got to live up to the expectations you set. What do you think is the number one mistake you see traders make?**

Todd:   I think trading without a defined plan, having unrealistic expectations and not being consistent with their process.

**Eddie: That was three things.**

Todd:   Discipline is huge. If you don't have discipline and patience... most of the time, you're waiting for the setup.

**Eddie: Right. So you're saying trading is not an active thing. A lot of trading is waiting.**

Todd:   Exactly. When the right setup comes, being able to pull that trigger and being able to follow your rules is paramount. When you're in a trade, the work should be over. What I mean by that is you've got the rules. You know exactly where your catastrophic stop is. You know where your logical profit targets are. If you're going to get into a trade for which you have no clue where it should go, then you probably shouldn't get into that trade. It's all about long-term probabilities. You've got to learn to think in long-term probabilities.

**Eddie: Tell me about expectations. I get a giant percentage of traders who are new. They think they know the market because they've purchased a stock in the past. What I've learned is that many times, their expectations are really out of whack. I speak to people who think they can take $10,000 and make a living with it right out of the gate.**

Todd:   Right.

**Eddie: Do you have things you tell people to temper them of those expectations?**

Todd:   I give them the analogy of becoming a doctor or a lawyer. It takes time. They go through schooling, practice, an internship. This is pretty much the same thing, don't you agree?

**Eddie: Yeah. You can't become a doctor at a seminar.**

Todd:  Exactly. Just because you read a book or go through a program doesn't mean that you can immediately make a living by trading. You've got to take what you learn, internalize it and make it your own. It's got to mesh with your personality, temperament, time constraints and risk level.

**Eddie: Experience. The experience of the emotions that you go through as a trader; it really takes years to learn how to temper those emotions.**

Todd:  Right.

**Eddie: You and I, we've been at this a long time. Trading is the kind of activity that will bring up all your personal baggage. I think that's one of the things that traders struggle with the most: the emotions.**

Todd:  Emotions are very important. 90% of trading is discipline, but if you don't have a methodology with an edge, with that positive expectancy, you can have the greatest discipline for being a trader and you still won't make money. You need to be able to control your emotions.

**Eddie: What would you say is your best piece of advice for somebody who wants to learn trading?**

Todd:   You need to find somebody that's actually making a living doing it, and really try to model them. Don't start trading with live money. You also need to get the proper education. Always use stops, of course, when you do enter a market.

**Eddie: Right.**

Todd:   Know your loss beforehand. Assume that you've lost your money before you begin trading. If you start a $10,000 account, assume it's not there. You've got to be detached from the money.

**Eddie: How do you do that? How do you stay detached?**

Todd:   I just don't think of it.

**Eddie: Is there a daily practice? Obviously, in the beginning, it took some practice to get to where you are now, emotionally and mentally. Was there some technique that you used?**

Todd:   I do have some visualization exercises that I do in the morning; visualizing how I'm making money. I really try to get into that Zen state.

**Eddie: I can totally relate to you, Todd, because you've been at it for so long. Like me, you've reached a stage of expertise. Have you ever met somebody**

**who's an expert at something, and when you meet them they're talking too far ahead of what you can comprehend? I get you because I've been trading for a long time, like you.**

Todd: You hit the nail on the head. I've been doing this for so long, it's so second nature to me. It's hard to summarize trading in a couple of sentences.

**Eddie: You and I have never met before, and I know I'm coming out of right field with some of these questions. I think this is an excellent conversation we're having.**

Todd: Good questions, too. I appreciate it.

**Eddie: If people want to learn about what you teach, how can people learn about you?**

Todd: Go to TradingConceptsInc.com. It's got all of the programs, and information about me and Doc. Call me up. I love talking to traders.

**Eddie: So, you're easily accessible?**

Todd: I'm very easily accessible. That's been my mantra for the last 20 years. I think I can teach people effectively. I think this business, if you're not guided, you can spend years trying to figure it out.

**Eddie: Right.**

Todd: You can get that analysis paralysis.

**Eddie: Absolutely.**

Todd:   Buy all the books and courses.

**Eddie: And the indicators.**

Todd:   There are hundreds of indicators and millions of variations. I'm a huge price action guy. You've got to understand price and the natural rhythm of the market before you try to apply any type of technical indicator on top of your chart. You need to learn how to read the tape.

**Eddie: Right. What does reading the tape mean to you?**

Todd:   Reading a naked chart with nothing on it. You need to understand what it's doing at all times. The market is never going to lie.

From 1995-2000, the people I spoke with that were trying to short that market, thinking that the market couldn't go any higher—if you look at a weekly price chart of the S&Ps from 1995 to 2000, at the most you had two weeks that made lower highs and lower lows.

People trying to go against that and getting their clock cleaned... I heard all the stories.

**Eddie: Sure.**

Todd:   Why fight it?

**Eddie: Todd, I really appreciate you taking the time to do this interview. If readers and listeners are interested in learning more about Trading Concepts, visit TradingConceptsInc.com.**

**Todd's Key Secrets to Remember:**

1. Emotions are very important. 90% of trading is discipline, but if you don't have a methodology with an edge, you can have the greatest discipline for being a trader and you still won't make money. You need to be able to control your emotions.

2. Model your career after a successful trader.

3. Know your loss beforehand. Assume you've lost your money before you begin trading. You've got to be detached from your money.

# Markus Heitkoetter

Markus Heitkoetter is a former IBM director who quit his job and moved from Germany to Texas in 2002. He became a full-time trader, and in 2005 founded Rockwell Trading in order to simplify the trading process. He is the author of the bestselling *The Simple Strategy*, which helps traders improve their trading with a simple, easy-to-use trading method.

**Eddie: The first question I want to ask you, Markus, is when and how did you get into trading?**

Markus: This was way back in 1989. I was about to finish high school and I was fascinated by trading. Now, being in high school, I used all my disposable income, which was 50 Deutsche Marks because I am from Germany (these days, equivalent to about $50). I bought one share of V.W., Volkswagen, the car manufacturer.

There weren't any brokers in 1989, so you had to go to a bank. I opened a brokerage account with Deutsche Bank. The next day in school as soon as there was a break, I ran to a pay phone and called my broker. How was my one share doing? He said it had gone up a few cents. I was ecstatic.

I called him again at the second break in school, and as soon as I'd gotten home. I did that every day for three days, until my broker asked me how much I wanted to make on that stock. I said a gain of 20% (approximately $10) would be fantastic. My broker said he'd pay me the $10 gain to stop calling him three times a day. So, my first trade was a profitable trade.

**Eddie: What about after that? How do you get into it as a part-time to full-time endeavor?**

Markus: I quickly realized that with my account of 50 Deutsche Mark, I couldn't do a whole lot. So, I saved more money and then started trading options. My trades were mostly straddles and strangles right ahead of earnings. I thought that after earnings were announced, the stock would move one way or the other. This was the game I was playing and I did fairly well. I did this all the way through college.

After college, when I told my parents that I wanted to be a full-time trader, they encouraged me to do something that really earns a living.

I used to work for IBM in Germany for several years, and traded in the evenings. Finally, in 2002, I got burned out. I decided to leave IBM, and move from Germany to the U.S. to become a full-time trader.

**Eddie: During those early years with the options trading, did you have a mentor? Did you have a system? How did you learn how to get into straddles and strangles?**

Markus: I learned a lot from books that I got from the local library. I didn't attend any seminars at this point, and there were no DVDs. When I did the options trading, a lot of the knowledge came from books.

**Eddie: I would imagine there was a lot of trial and error because you really didn't have anyone to ask questions.**

Markus: I thought there was this one magic trading system or indicator that would take my account to the next level; that it could even be automated. I wasted three years of my life trying to automate trading systems. This was in '96 when computers were very slow. I used end-of-day data that I downloaded from a server, and then the computer was running all night trying to spit out the hot stock picks.

You and I know that it is not that easy.

**Eddie: When you first got started, how profitable were you?**

Markus: In the beginning, it was a lot of hit and miss. I had a few good trades that took my account to the next level, but then I made some stupid mistakes and wiped out three trading accounts. Talking to many other professional traders, it seems this is the path that most professional traders follow.

**Eddie: What size accounts were they, if you don't mind me asking?**

Markus: They were anywhere between $10,000-$25,000. Beginner accounts, definitely.

**Eddie: Right, but you definitely blew up $30,000+ during the learning curve.**

Markus: Absolutely. Trading in options, I was selling—I think it was a trade in the bonds—right before the first Iraq war, when everyone was thinking it'd be over quickly. Needless to say it wasn't over quickly and bonds went the wrong way. This was one of the trades that wiped out my account in a single trade.

**Eddie: So, you had big losses in the beginning. You had several accounts that blew up. What kept you motivated to keep trying?**

Markus: I'd heard of successful traders. I knew that it was possible. I thought, I should be able to figure it out. The secret to trading is not the latest indicator or the latest trading strategy. It is about evaluating what works and what doesn't.

**Eddie: Can you explain that?**

Markus: It's like in business. Having my IBM background, when I moved to the U.S. in 2002, I started keeping trading logs because I wanted to see which of the trades were working and which didn't. I started analyzing my own trades. I figured out that I was doing really well trading the indices and the bonds, but that I was a lousy currency trader. I was trading six markets at the time and I noticed that I made money in four markets. Therefore, one of the ways to improve my trading was to stop trading the consistent losers.

Another thing that I figured out is that I am a better trader if I trade in the morning, so I stopped trading in the afternoon. I still maintain and analyze these logs today, to continue to see what is most effective for me. I'm approaching it more from a business perspective than a trading perspective.

**Eddie: Interesting. It sounds like you were doing some over-trading or trying to play too many games at the same time.**

Markus: Definitely. After I moved to the U.S. to become a full-time trader, this is when somebody told me—I think it must have been my broker—that you need to make at least 100 trades a day to be a day trader.

**Eddie: Oh my goodness.**

Markus: Exactly. However, making that many trades gave me an opportunity to evaluate these trading logs and then to realize I was heavily over-trading. Also, switching from a smaller timeframe to a larger timeframe has definitely helped my trading. The only way I could get 100 trades in a day was if I was trading on one- and three-minute charts.

**Eddie: Why do you think it is that you trade best in the morning?**

Markus: I think over-trading is a common disease amongst traders because we're all driven by greed and fear. Every trading system has a series of winning trades, but there's also a series of losing trades. It's helped me tremendously to work with daily and weekly goals. I set how much money I want to make with trading, then break it down into monthly, weekly, and daily goals.

Once I've achieved my daily goal, I stop trading; sometimes that's after a few minutes. That's tough for a trader because we're all addicted to watching charts. It's really tough to switch off the charts after just a few minutes, but I notice this helps me dramatically.

**Eddie: Right. What would you say are the secrets to journaling or keeping a log? What information is most important? Then, how do you do the analysis?**

Markus: The columns I have in my trading log are the date, the market that I'm trading, whether I go long or short (because I like to play both sides of the market), the entry time, the price, the exit time, and the exit price. I've found on more than one occasion that my long trades work out much better. By recording the times, I see how long I am staying in a trade and what time of day I made the trade. If I see that I'm in a trade for longer than 20 minutes, it usually turns into a losing trade.

For me, with my trading style, the winning trades occur rather quickly. This is why, in addition to having a profit target and stop loss, I also use a time stop.

**Eddie: You close out even if it's moving in your direction?**

Markus: Yes, because there's always a possibility of the trade turning around.

**Eddie: Of course.**

Markus: I'd rather exit a trade with a small profit than with a large loss. In addition to this, I am a firm believer in trading multiple trading strategies. I want to see which of the trading strategies is outperforming the market right now.

**Eddie: You came to the United States in 2002, specifically to focus on being a trader. How'd that go? Tell us about that.**

Markus: When I first became a full-time trader, it was starkly different because I had the entire day to do with what I pleased. I could follow the markets all day, and I believed that was the missing piece. It didn't go as smoothly in the beginning as I hoped, which taught me to log everything.

I was sitting in front of the computer almost all day. I did a lot of live trading, simulated trading, and back testing because I wanted to get as many trades in as possible. It really took me a few months before it clicked. To date, I still love to look at all sorts of strategies. I'm a very active trader; I don't like sitting on my hands, waiting for opportunities. This is why I'm trading multiple strategies on multiple markets.

Now, there are other strategies for which you have to be more patient; that is not for me. This is why I tell new traders that whenever you get a new strategy, make sure it fits your trading personality.

**Eddie: Right. During that period, you were trying to get in your 100 trades a day. I know I already asked this, but was there a mentor? Was there one person who you had access to, who was making money, who was showing you some strategies?**

Markus: My trading was definitely influenced by quite a few successful traders, such as Van Tharp (in terms of risk management), John Bollinger (I still use 'Bollinger Bands' to date), Joe Ross, and Larry Williams (his way of analyzing the markets). Needless to say, Mark Douglas' books about the 'Disciplined Trader' classics and Jack Schwager's *Market Wizards* were big influences. I think there's a lot of information that Jack extracts from these professional traders in the same way you do it here, in this series.

**Eddie: Excellent. Tell me about the strategies that consistently work for you. Is it a set of strategies that consistently work? It sounds like it's ever-evolving for you.**

Markus: Yes, but I have a core set of strategies. The first is a trend-following strategy. Now, trend-following strategies are great because you risk a little to make more, so with this strategy I like to risk $100 to make $150. If the market is trending, this is a great strategy. However, as we know, the markets are not always trending. Another strategy that I use is a scalping strategy. What I like about scalping strategies is that they have a very high winning percentage. My first trades in the mornings are always with a scalping strategy, because even though the profits are small, it helps me psychologically. Especially right after the markets open, they're just bouncing around, so they're perfect for scalp trades.

**Eddie: Are you mainly still trading with options?**

Markus: No, I'm actively trading the futures markets. For my day trading, I'm trading the futures markets. I'm looking at the E-mini S&P, the DOW, and the NASDAQ. I also like to trade crude oil, gold, the Euro, and the bond. These are the eight markets that I watch. I also do a little options and stock trading, but I would say the majority of my trading is day trading the futures markets.

**Eddie: Can you give us a little more color on your scalping strategy?**

Markus: The scalping strategy is actually fairly simple. All I try to do is buy at the low of the previous bar, and sell at the high of the previous bar. I like to use range bars, so I'm not using any time-based charts.

As an example, in the E-mini S&P, it's more or less a reversion to the mean strategy, that after the market moves two points in one direction, it usually retracts by half a point.

**Eddie: How are you defining the range of the bar if it's not time-based?**

Markus: The range of the bar is based on the volatility of the market. I look at how much a market moves on average from the high of the day to the low of the day. It's like the ATR (the average true range). For my range bars, I use between 10-12% because I like a multiple of four.

**Eddie: If someone wanted to learn about these strategies, where could they learn about it?**

Markus: I have a website, RockwellTrading.com. There's a lot of free information there. I believe I even mentioned the trading strategies for free there. I have published a Kindle book, so for $1 you get the detailed rules of the strategy. I love to share the strategies because they're solid.

**Eddie: Everyone's going to follow those rules in a different way or interpret them in a different way, so these strategies can be used by many and not overlap. Do you teach live?**

Markus: I sometimes teach live, but it's usually just once a year. A lot of my materials are available either as books or DVDs. Usually once a year, I teach in front of a small group.

**Eddie: You have a lot of information that you give away for free. You have a lot of excellent course material as well on RockwellTrading.com. I'm sure you get asked many questions. What would you say is the top question that traders ask you?**

Markus: "How much money can I make with trading?"

**Eddie: What's your answer for that?**

Markus: I think, realistically, you should shoot for 40-60% per year. In trading, the more risk you take, the more money you can make. If you want to risk, say, approximately the Two Percent Rule (2% per trade), then you should realistically expect anywhere from 40-60% a year. All these websites that claim you can get started with $10,000 and make $1.6 million the next year, I don't believe in that. I'm all about realistic expectations.

My next most-asked question is "What is the best trading strategy?" The best trading strategy is the one that is making you money.

**Eddie: Right.**

Markus: I encourage every trader to try out different strategies. Get at least 40 trades in so that you have statistically relevant data that you can then analyze. Unfortunately, most traders go from one shiny object to the next. I think you should test any strategy, no matter where you're getting it from, over at least 40 trades to get a statistically relevant sample.

**Eddie: You definitely bring in an engineering type of analytics to do what you do, but you also incorporate the psychology at the same time. That's pretty unique, and I think traders listening and reading should really take that into account. It is analyzing, almost in an engineering way, your own behavior.**

Markus: Yes.

**Eddie: I think that's a very important point you're making.**

Markus: You summarized it perfectly, because once I made the switch from chasing the latest strategy to analyzing my trades and myself, this is when my trading turned around.

**Eddie: I try to tell my people all the time that it's really about what's going on in between your ears more than anything. Unfortunately, when we first learn about trading, it is a shiny object. There is**

**this overwhelming hope of getting rich quickly. There is a learning curve, then success definitely comes from being able to have the patience to go through the hours of figuring it out and analyzing yourself.**

Markus: Exactly.

**Eddie: I'm going to use a sports analogy. I live in Miami and one of our great basketball players is Dwyane Wade. He just is not a good three point shooter; he's really come to know this and he just doesn't take that shot because he knows that shot doesn't work for him.**

**I think as traders, we don't focus on the things that we're really good at. They talk about, when you do some type of self analysis, looking at the things you're not good at and trying to get better at them. I would argue that you should take a look at the things you are good at and focus more on getting better at those things.**

Markus: I absolutely agree. As I said earlier, I noticed in the beginning that the Euro was not my market. I then had two options: I could either keep banging my head against the wall, or embrace the five other markets I was succeeding in.

**Eddie:** That, in my opinion, is one mistake that a lot of new traders make: wasting time trying to figure that market out when they could be focusing on the things they have figured out. Just focus on your goal, to find the system that makes money for you and be good at that. Really, isn't it your ultimate goal to make money and feel stress free doing it?

Markus: Absolutely. Don't get me wrong, I'm not saying you don't need strategies, but the important thing is with every strategy that you learn and test. I think it's very important to learn from each strategy to really chisel out what kind of trader you are.

**Eddie:** Right. What is the top question that you wish students and new traders would ask you?

Markus: I think the most important question that I would like to be asked by aspiring traders is, "What does it really take to become a trader? What are your realistic expectations in terms of the time and money I'll need, and what are the results you think I can achieve?"

**Eddie: What's your answer?**

Markus: It takes several hundred trades, possibly even a few thousand trades—it can be in a simulated environment—to figure out what type of trader you are and what strategies you need. I firmly believe that in order to get started with trading, you need to have at least a $10,000 account. Having said that, if you start with a $10,000 account, you cannot expect to make a living with trading after two or three months. You should be happy if you can increase this $10,000 account. Approach trading systematically. Keep trading logs to make sure that you learn from the mistakes you're making and from the trades that worked. Why did they work?

**Eddie: You would call that your best piece of advice to someone who wants to learn trading?**

Markus: Yes, definitely.

**Eddie: What would be your best piece of advice to a trader who's taken a big loss?**

Markus: Take a few days off. After a big loss, your confidence is shaken and there are two possible scenarios: you're now afraid to place the next trade, or you might have this fight instinct during which you're over-trading and making stupid mistakes.

**Eddie: Revenge trading.**

Markus: Exactly. If you fall off the horse, you do need to get back on, but do you have to do it immediately or do you take your time? I recommend taking the time.

**Eddie: There's a lot of buzz on television these days about computerized trading and high frequency trading. Do you believe all the buzz is warranted? Do you think it has a negative effect on your ability to make money in the markets?**

Markus: First of all, there's no doubt that computers have changed the way we trade. I remember when I started trading, I had to call in the orders to an order desk or to a broker, who then submitted it to an order desk, who then gave it to a runner who went into the pit. It took 15 minutes. Now, it is instantaneous.

Now, it appears that high frequency traders have found a loophole to un-level the playing field again, where they front run you. Fortunately, this is not the case in the futures markets that I'm trading. Therefore, the high frequency trading doesn't have an effect on my personal trading. High frequency trading is done in the stock market and I believe to some extent it might be able to do it in the options market. From what I understand, it's mainly the stock market.

**Eddie: Okay. If you had to say your absolute favorite strategy and/or favorite market, what would it be?**

Markus: It is definitely the trend-following strategy. In terms of market, this changes frequently. Right now, as we are recording this interview in February 2015, the crude oil market has been a fantastic market to trade in because it shows the longer lasting trend throughout the day. Even the stock indices have been great to trade intraday. As a day trader, I love volatile markets and I believe that this year, we had more triple digit moves in the DOW than we have had in a long time, and that is fantastic for a day trader. However, if this volatility decreases again—and it could decrease both in crude oil and in the markets— I might switch over to gold and the Euro currency. My favorite market is a market that moves; a volatile market.

**Eddie: Right. The futures markets open earlier than the stock market does, if you're trading the indices and some of the futures markets. I know crude and at the commodities markets, they trade overnight.**

Markus: Yes.

**Eddie: You run strategies overnight?**

Markus: No, I trade the markets shortly after the real market opening (9:30am EST). Even though the markets are trading 24 hours, most of the time there's not much going on in the overnight session. The markets are really getting an impulse once the New York Stock Exchange opens. I need to have volume and volatility for successful trades.

**Eddie: How do the gap openings affect you?**

Markus: Fortunately, since I open and close a position within a day, I'm not affected by gaps.

**Eddie: I know from looking at your website, you have a free book. Can you tell us about that?**

Markus: It's a free e-book, *The Complete Guide to Day Trading*. I wrote this a few years ago but the content, I believe, is timeless. You can download it right now from my website. It's close to 300 pages and covers pretty much everything that we talked about today.

How much money can I make with trading? What is the best way to get started? What timeframe should I use? Should I day trade or should I swing trade? I answer all these questions and more.

**Eddie: You have another book on Amazon for $0.99. What's the name of that book?**

Markus: That is *The Simple Strategy*, which is about my favorite strategy, the trend-following strategy. Now, this works very well in the futures markets but it also works for Forex traders and stock traders. I explained the exact rules in this book.

**Eddie: So, people can get a download of your strategies, what you've learned over all these years of**

**trading, for $0.99. If people go to your website, it will direct them to the book on Amazon, correct?**

Markus: Absolutely. It is on the home page.

**Eddie: Now, what are some of the other items, services and teachings that you offer?**

Markus: I think the most valuable thing I have to offer is the Rockwell Trading Club; this is where I put all of my trading strategies in the member-protected website. Over the years, I have traded 18 different strategies. In addition to the four core strategies that I use, there are 14 other strategies that I have been trading and that I regularly trade depending on the market conditions. All this is in the member section of the website and you can have it for a low monthly fee.

I'm not trying to make a lot of money with this. I just love trading and I need to pay my support staff, so that's why I am charging a slight cost for it.

**Eddie: There are some other videos in there as well?**

Markus: There are videos about money management, trading psychology, how to structure trading as a business, etcetera.

**Eddie: It sounds very complete.**

Markus: That was my goal with it, because when I started trading I had to read all these books and it seems that in each book only one aspect of trading was covered. With the Rockwell Trading Club, my goal is to have the most comprehensive library where you find everything you need.

**Eddie: Is there anything else you would like to add or say for this interview?**

Markus: Make sure you have a fast computer.

**Eddie: Good answer!**

Markus: There's so much data flying in as the markets are getting more volatile. You cannot afford, especially as a day trader, to lose ticks or wait on your computer. Make sure that you have the knowledge, then also the tools to execute the strategies.

**Eddie: Excellent. Just out of curiosity, did you ever automate any of your strategies?**

Markus: In terms of automation, I believe in rule-based trading. I see the entry and exit signals, then I decide whether I take the signal or not in the context of the market.

**Eddie: I like that approach. I don't think anybody has yet to develop the ATM machine of the market, where you just turn on a strategy and it kicks out**

**money, even though there's people who claim to do that. I don't believe it's actually out there.**

Markus: No, me neither. It's very simple, because if you think about the big banks and brokerages who are still employing traders like Citibank & Goldman Sachs, spending millions of dollars each year on trader salaries. If they could buy a system for $97 that replaces millions of dollars in traders, they'd buy it, or by now they'd have developed it. They are employing the brightest minds in the industry and they still have traders trading the markets for the hedge funds.

**Eddie: That's right.**

Markus: None of them are automated. You always have a hedge fund manager that is responsible for placing these trades. Why believe a guy who's selling the Holy Grail for $97?

**Eddie: Excellent, Markus. I really appreciate you taking the time to do this interview. Again, if you want to check out all that Markus offers, visit RockwellTrading.com.**

**Markus' Key Secrets to Remember:**

1.  Having logs, keeping track of every trade to monitor what's working and what isn't, is very effective in helping you become a better trader.

2.  When you pick a trading strategy, make sure it fits your trading personality.

3.  It takes several hundred trades, possibly even a few thousand trades—it can be in a simulated environment —to figure out what type of trader you are and what strategies you need.

# Norman Hallett

Norman Hallett is the founder and CEO of Subconscious Training Corporation (STC). STC develops state-of-the-art mental training programs, including The Disciplined Trader Intensive Program, which is specifically designed to improve the psychology of trading.

Over his career, Norman has developed numerous successful startup companies, including the investment firm of Hallett Commodities, Inc., and the Introducing Broker operation, NCH Commodities, Inc. His fascination with the investment industry lead him to grow several firms in his 21-year career in the financial arena. His high-profile style resulted in his being a frequent guest of the Financial News Network, and culminated in his popular radio talk show, "Risky Business."

Norman is currently on a mission to get traders more disciplined.

**Eddie:** **Norman Hallett, also known as the disciplined trader. When and how did you get into trading, Norman?**

Norman: I started back in 1979. I was looking for a new career, and I started selling gold options on the telephone before there were actually exchange-traded options of any kind. All people could really do at that time was buy puts and calls on the actual physical metal from Mocatta Metals in London.

We advertised in various trading magazines, and I was on the phone explaining options, in their very basic form, to investors who wanted to take on gold and silver options.

**Eddie:** **It was an over-the-counter market. I can imagine the company you worked for must have made a market in those options?**

Norman: Actually, it was a private dealer option. Mocatta Metals actually made the market for us. Later on, Velour Whitewell out of Switzerland also made a market.

The great part about that experience was that the market zoomed to $850 in gold and $50 with the Hunt Brothers and silver. Those people who had $5,000-$10,000 investments all of a sudden were up at $100,000, $160,000 in a matter of four or five weeks. I said to myself, "What have I been doing all my life? I could have been helping all these people make all this money."

Of course, that experience was tempered months later as people didn't take their profits; they wound up with doubles and triples instead of the 15-20 times they would have had if they'd scaled out. That was my first dose of how greedy traders can be, and how out of control a broker can be by not suggesting people keep their feet on the ground. That was my first infusion of how important mental and emotional conditioning is.

**Eddie: Where did you go from there?**

Norman: I was with that firm for quite a while and became part of management. In 1988, I left that firm, and in '89 joined Paine Webber, who hired me to raise money for their futures fund. I ran a room for them where we talked to investors about managing money in the futures department. What happened, though, is after about five or six months (during which I raised millions for them), their manager preceded to lose 10-15% in a very short period of time. They closed that fund and wanted me to then sell mutual funds.

I moved on from Paine Webber and had various IBs. I worked for an IB and then I had my own IB; it all wound up as focusing on being a CTA. I had my own CTA operation where I managed several million dollars in the commodity field.

**Eddie: What does CTA stand for?**

Norman: Commodity trading advisor. A person who's licensed to take money and trade it on someone else's behalf. That was a designation I was proud of, and I did a pretty good job in that field for several years.

**Eddie: Now, did you trade your own money when you started managing other people's money?**

Norman: I've always had an open account. I traded my money alongside their money, but I could not trade the same things at the time. The laws were, you couldn't trade ahead of clients.

**Eddie: They were afraid of front-running.**

Norman: Right. You were better off just not trading those same things in your own account.

**Eddie: I'm curious about your own trading. You started in the gold, silver and metals doing options, then you moved on to raising money in commodities. When did you really start trading for your own account in commodities?**

Norman: I actually traded straight futures contracts when I was with the options firm. That was trading not only gold and silver, but also the agricultural and others. I really got my feet wet during that time. I had particular goals, but my trading plan wasn't anything like a professional one. Now you really can't go into the markets without a solid trading plan.

**Eddie: How long did it take you to figure out how to make money?**

Norman: I was up $100,000 then down $50,000, thinking I was the smartest guy on earth when I made money and the biggest idiot when I lost it. When I started as a professional CTA, that's really when I started to plan.

It was during that time that I had to get very strict, because as a commodity trading advisor you don't make any money unless your customers make money. You get a percentage of that profit. It became very easy to be disciplined from that standpoint. Then again, you're actually more emotional trading other people's money.

I've been married since 1981 to one of the world's most popular hypnotists. My wife Tisha, she's been on the cover of Hypnotist Magazine several times.

**Eddie: Sounds dangerous.**

Norman: That's what I thought at the time. I didn't give it the credibility that it deserved. She was smart, she was helping people, but I never thought that was something that I needed. It's those moments in time when you're not strong-willed that really identifies the winning traders from the losing traders. "I'm disciplined most of the time." That's probably the worst.

I asked my wife if she could help me to not short-circuit my trades. I would see my trades getting close to an area where I thought it would start to hesitate and was letting my emotions rule when to get out of these trades. I was leaving so much money on the table. I was jumping on trends but not following through.

So, I asked my wife to relax me and to use subconscious training to help me stay grounded and be disciplined with my trading. I was able to overcome fear and greed. I became a professional trader that was winning consistently. It was always from the mental work.

**Eddie:** **It sounds like you were catching trends as a trader, but you weren't letting them ride because you were too tense. Were you tense because you were taking some big losses, or because there was no consistency?**

Norman: All of those things happen when you don't have a plan and you're not emotionally fit to run that plan. This happened to me after I left Paine Webber. That's when I sought my wife's help. We would start every morning with a 20-minute session. Eventually, what my firm ended up doing was making bite-sized mental and emotional training sessions. I just sit up, take a few breaths, get the positive messages in. All of a sudden you're focused and ready to go.

Being consistent with the mental training and then journaling was paramount. Journaling is where you're honest with yourself. To this day, nobody reads my journals. I've learned not to beat myself up, I've learned to compliment myself.

*One Minute Manager* instructed managers to be upfront about issues in the workplace. Start with something the employee is doing right, then describe the problem, and finish with a compliment.

It's a criticism sandwich. If you start every conversation with pounding your employee, nothing's going to get better. It's the same thing in trading.

I've brought that to every training I do now. I'm a wise and disciplined trader, and I do the things that a wise and disciplined trader does.

You have positive feelings about the future, you know the importance of staying on task with your trading plan, and you've identified yourself as wise. That is really the core of what I train people to do today.

**Eddie: So, the mental training you teach now was all developed out of your own need for it; you were very fortunate to marry somebody who was an expert at mental training. You were able to apply what she learned to your own situation.**

Norman: I'm lucky in that we have immense respect for each other. I'm living with somebody who understands the importance of not hiding your emotions, but controlling your emotions and directing your thoughts in a positive way. We have a rule that we don't yell at each other. She won't even listen to the news.

**Eddie: You're from New York, and you don't yell?**

Norman: She's from California.

**Eddie: That makes sense.**

Norman: Exactly, Eddie, that's it.

**Eddie: Mental training is a big part of what you do. Can you describe what mental training is from a trader's perspective?**

Norman: It's all about your subconscious mind. We make our decisions consciously. When we get a signal to take a trade from our trading plan, our conscious mind asks whether to take the trade. The answer to that question is based on what is held true for the subconscious mind, and it's done in a split second.

What happens is when that trade gets instigated, when you hesitate to take that trade, that means you're making decisions based on a subconscious belief that it's not in your best interest.

**Eddie: How does a trader recognize if they have any of these mental blocks?**

Norman: It's very easy. Your actions tell you what your subconscious dominant beliefs are. If you're hesitating to make a decision, if you're feeling fear and greed, these are qualities that somehow your subconscious mind is holding as beneficial to you.

Now, how do you change a poor behavioral subconscious structure to one that will serve you as a trader? The mental training that I talked about. It puts your conscious mind to the side and allows this neural pathway to be delivered to your subconscious mind. If you relax yourself and think *I'm a wise and disciplined trader and I do the things that a wise and a disciplined trader does*, what happens is you're collecting and multiplying these neural pathways into a dominant behavior.

Essentially, you're creating neural pathways with the beliefs that benefit you as a trader. It doesn't take long; a 7-minute session every day for two weeks will do it. It becomes second nature, just as hesitating and worrying became second nature.

**Eddie: So, you have these old behaviors subconsciously networked in your mind, they're default settings of your psyche, and you're going to try to replace them with new ones that are more conducive to trading.**

Norman: Right. The conscious mind makes decisions based on what the subconscious mind holds true for you. The other function of the conscious mind is to defend your beliefs.

You have to understand the process as simple as I've explained it. Test that process. You must be patient. I find that patience is the one talent or skill that a trader, when they develop that, makes the biggest change from struggle to profitability.

**Eddie: When you first start as a trader, patience is not on your mind; you're looking for instant gratification. Also, trading will bring every negative belief you have about yourself to the surface. It really is a great way to work on yourself.**

Norman: It works in every part of your life. On our site, people stay with us long after they become great and disciplined traders. I put in a section a couple of years ago with sessions on being a better golfer, tennis player, etcetera. There's 75 different mental training sessions for other parts of your life.

**Eddie: I'm going to mention three terms, and you tell me whether there's a difference between them: mental training, hypnosis, and mental rehearsal.**

Norman: They all fall into the category of "helpful." I would say that mental training and hypnosis... we don't use the H word.

**Eddie: It has a negative connotation.**

Norman: That's right, it comes with baggage, it comes with stage hypnotism. So, we use "mental training" or "subconscious training" because it's a softer term, but it really is self-hypnosis. When you miss your exit on the freeway, when you mindlessly watch a TV show you don't like; you zone out. It's a very relaxing state and you do it to yourself all the time. That's why Super Bowl commercials are so expensive, because they know they've got a ready crowd to be mentally trained, really.

**Eddie: You could definitely argue that the TV networks, they understand that they already have you**

**completely hypnotized and they're expert at planting messages.**

Norman: The beauty of self-hypnosis is that you get to put into your subconscious mind exactly what you want. The other term that can be used is "subliminal suggestions."

In self-hypnosis you create what you want. The way you structure your sentences is important. For example, saying, "I will not miss my trades anymore," is not the way you want to suggest to your subconscious mind because without the word "not," the whole message falls apart. You'd be better off saying, "I will take every trade with confidence."

**Eddie: It's been proven that terrorism, fires, floods, all these horrible things, actually excite our brain and will capture your attention. Commercials incorporating these are more effective.**

Norman: You're right. They sell you the solution. The idea of self-hypnosis is that you can actually build the exact person that you want to be, with the exact skills and talents that you want. That's a proven fact. I've done it for myself.

**Eddie: Do you find that traders usually come to you when they've reached a point of pain? It's**

**become so excruciating that they're giving up that they need help of some sort?**

Norman: Yes. There's a 7% refund rate on our products and services, and the vast majority of that 7% are traders who came to us with only one or two trades left in their account. I couldn't get them to take the sessions quickly enough. What good is mental toughness and mental fitness if you're using it to run a trading plan that's not sound? We get into how to make sure you've got the right money and risk management. We realize that the best gain is not losing money.

**Eddie: Where does journaling come into mental training?**

Norman: I find that it's synergistic with mental trainings. It's a place to be honest with yourself. I was in Egypt and I bought three or four journals. I have some that are unique leather from London. I honor these; when I open it up, I'm writing another page in my life.

What is a good statement I can make to launch myself tomorrow? It's inspiring, it starts the control process, it puts you into control. I find that the dominant thought of new traders about the market is that the market is in control; that you are a victim of where the market takes you.

There is some truth to that last part, but you ultimately have the control. You have the control of how much you're willing to risk. The truth is, that's enough to get you where you want to go. You don't have to control the price action; you can just analyze the price action.

The journaling helps you to identify where your trading plan may need help, where your mental and emotional skills may need help. The most impatient person can be patient.

**Eddie:** **Clearly you're passionate about the concept of mental training and how it can improve your life and your trading. Tell me about your website and the products you have.**

Norman: I give a lot of free stuff to my people and I want them to get comfortable with the idea that they're in control. I talk a lot about positive expectancy. I think that you have to expect a positive future in order to get one.

At TheDisciplinedTrader.com, we offer one program that has it all. It starts with instruction on making sure that you have a proper trading plan. Another module covers risk and money management, another covers journaling, and there's one done by a friend of mine, Joe Ross.

Joe Ross is a monster trader and a terrific person. He's all about framing your trading as a business; taking it seriously. Losses are costs of business, wins are profits. This way, if you have a profitable business, you're not so willing to give it away. Somehow, people think you can risk money currently in the market more loosely, because that's the market's money. When you make a profit, you have to defend it.

We start with that and then we move on to what I consider the most important part: it's a matter of training your mind to develop the simple skills so that you can follow your trading plan without hesitation, overcoming fear and greed, developing patience. You're there to make money.

**Eddie: I find that lots of traders get so hung up on the need to be right that they lose track of why they're there.**

Norman: It's okay to want to be right, but *why* do you want to be right?

We talk about stopping the hesitation to pull the trigger on your trades. Pull the trigger and don't move your stops around. Be happy to take your losses, because the losses are designed to help you.

You've got to put the wins and the losses behind you. It's just a constant forward motion as a trader.

That's what the course is all about: making sure you have the structure and the proper respect for risk and money management.

**Eddie: It sounds a lot like law of attraction; setting up your mind to have a positive expectancy. Do you use that term at all?**

Norman: I don't use it much, because I'd like to see more about taking action, not just putting out thought and expecting all of the answers to come back.

What will come back to you when you put out positive thoughts are options and choices. When you make a bad decision, you'll continue with that positive thought, focusing on where you want to be. You can't always get from Point A to Point B with Plan A and no deviation. We adjust constantly.

They've studied MRIs of the brain and found that when you have a thought, there is energy that is expelled. We all know that energy is never created or destroyed. It just continues to transition.

**Eddie: Where does neurolinguistic programming come in?**

Norman: NLP describes the attempt to get to the same place with different technique. NLP is all about giving more thought energy to what you want and less thought energy to what you don't want. In other words, you de-emphasize when negative thoughts come up, and you emphasize things that you do want.

NLP uses different ways to send those neural pathways to the subconscious mind. It uses touch and thought, which is one reason I liked journaling. When you're writing, you're making neural pathways that are created through kinesthetic motion, the pencil to the paper. I actually whisper to myself while I'm writing, so I get visual and audio.

I'm getting different processes with different neural pathways, which are bringing the subconscious mind the energy to form that neuro-net that represents what I want to be as a trader and as a person.

There's another thing that's out there, called thought-filled therapy (TFT). It was developed by somebody who used to charge $30,000 to other therapists to train under him. Nowadays, it's evolved into the tapping solution. Literally what you're doing is having thoughts, and at the same time, tapping acupressure points. They've found that this allows you to take emotions out of a thought.

**Eddie: It's medically proven?**

Norman: The problem is that if you want to quantify, if you want to put it under the medically proven, you've got to have a $50 million study. Most of these new age and new energy people are not capable of that. It's true of even medicines now, they can't get approval and they're doing it in Europe. All I can say is that in the tapping solution, TFT, the point is that you're not taking any pills.

Within 10 minutes, sometimes 15-20 minutes, this series of tapping takes the emotion out of thoughts. It's used for grief counseling, for people who are having suicidal thoughts. All of a sudden you have the thought come up and there's no negative emotion in it.

**Eddie: Do you have information about that on your website?**

Norman: Yes. It's part of what we do for those who want to work with that.

**Eddie: The last term I'm going to mention to you is meditation. How is this the same or different than Buddhist meditation, for example?**

Norman: I don't think I've ever had an interview quite like this; these are excellent questions. Meditation is a travel inward, really. I don't see it as a creative process, I see it as an acceptance process. We have everything that we need to be happy. We need to be accepting of who we are, where we've come from, the positive person that we are, the loving person that we've become, and meditation is all about turning inward and developing that inner confidence which translates later into an inner strength that allows you to do all of the things that we've already discussed.

Meditation is the general tonic. The truth is, and any wise man will tell you, you already have all the answers.

**Eddie: Wow. As a trainer and teacher, what is the top question students ask you?**

Norman: "How do I stop taking big losses?" There's usually one or two things that they're doing consistently which is ruining their trading results. They're cutting their profits short and letting their losses run, or they move a stop, or they start telling themselves stories of grandeur.

The one problem that's usually hurting new traders is that they consistently win, and then they have a big loss that wipes it all out and more. Then they revenge trade.

To me, it's all about helping them make the transition to a successful, effective trading plan. We try to reverse the most dominant problem.

We have an array of different mental training sessions, six basic core ones, and although they're in a certain order, you can jump to module five and just drill on that particular training.

That's how we do it, because I find that traders don't have much patience and if I can't get results for them early in our relationship, they're going to allow another type of emotion to drive them to whatever the next best trade is. It's all about giving yourself power.

**Eddie:** **I find that people have no idea about the emotional onslaught that comes with trading. They're about to experience emotions they never even knew existed, and some of them don't show up for years.**

**If somebody was to visit your website for the first time, how would you walk them through it?**

Norman: TheDisciplinedTrader.com. We have so many good, free giveaways right now, I think we're giving away the digital copy of my book *How to Build a Responsible Trading Plan.* We're also giving away other PDFs that can help you along. I want people to be comfortable with it. I send emails to my list almost on a daily basis, and my traders allow me to do that because I'm not sending them fluff, I'm sending them specific thoughts. Every week I come out with a four-minute drill that's posted on YouTube and it's delivered into the mailbox of anybody that's downloaded any of that free stuff or subscribed.

**Eddie: What is that?**

Norman: This week is the 177th week of the four-minute drill.

Basically, I deliver a message to you, an uplifting message. Describe the problem or the situation, then I give you the solution to that situation and the possible mental training you should take.

At the end, I always say "stay disciplined." There are people who watch me for a year on these four-minute drills and then I'll get an email from them and at the end of the email they'll say "stay disciplined" right back to me.

A forum just doesn't cut it. Sometimes you have to have a little club and know that you're going to get the mental and emotional support. Download any of our free stuff and that will automatically put you on the list.

**Eddie: I subscribe to your list. I watch your four-minute drills and I'm very much about mental rehearsal and mental training. Thank you for the work that you've done, and thanks for doing this**

**interview. Is there any final thing you wanted to add?**

Norman: I appreciate it. It's the quietest part of a trader's development, the mental and emotional, and yet it's got to be the most important. I think any professional trader that's had any long-term success will tell you that the most important thing is your mental and emotional fitness.

There's such a need in the trading community that we focus 100% now on helping traders, but years ago we helped golfers. In fact, for a time, our software was required for the Royal Academy of Tennis in Canada. This was 10 or 15 years ago.

We have to see ourselves as trading athletes, as money athletes. I think if you frame it like that, it can become a very exciting thing. Eddie, thanks for the opportunity, and to everybody reading/listening: stay disciplined.

**Eddie: Thank you so much, Norman.**

**Norman's Key Secrets to Remember:**

1.  The importance of controlling your emotions and directing your thoughts in a positive way, for a trader, is imperative for success.

2. Being kind to yourself helps you to be successful.

3. Journalling is the one unbiased way to be honest with yourself. No holding back; lay it all out there, and that will help you to objectively refine your trading system.

# Rob Booker

Rob Booker is a forex trader, best-selling author, trading educator and creator of the Traders Podcast. He has created numerous courses for traders with his unique style and fun personality. As Rob says on his website RobBooker.com, "I make stuff for traders. I teach traders to make more money, and have more fun."

**Eddie: When did you get into trading, Rob, and how?**

Rob: I got into trading in an average way. I was in a financial back-against-the-wall position, which is exactly where you shouldn't be. In 2000, I had run my first business into the ground. We had lost all the money that we put into it. At one point, Eddie, we were bringing in $70,000 a month.

Unfortunately, we were spending $80,000 a month. As any business person knows, that's a terrible way to run a business. I was left with about $150,000 of debt.

I decided I was going to try to make it up. I called a friend in San Francisco, who was the Head of Correspondent Clearing at Bear Stearns. He, essentially, was the liaison with hedge funds and they cleared all the trades for about 25 hedge funds. I told him I was thinking about doing some trading to make quick cash. I'm not embarrassed to admit that I was like everyone else in the way that I saw these spectacular returns that these hedge funds produced and thought I could do it too.

**Eddie: I think that's what attracts many people to the markets; this idea of getting rich quick.**

Rob:    I've spent my years saying that's a bad idea, but I've got to admit, everybody successful that I've met in this business—including myself—started with that same perspective.

Ron Suber of Bear Stearns told me I could get into trading, but warned me against foreign exchange. He said the leverage was out of control and the market was completely unregulated.

Of course, all the check boxes for how to make a lot of money in a short time were being ticked off. No

regulation, very high leverage, massive volatility…
check. I opened my first trading account in foreign
exchange. That's how I got started.

**Eddie: As soon as he said, "Don't do this," you couldn't
resist.**

Rob:    I've been a counter-trend trader ever since. I'm a
complete contrarian. I'm proud of it. It's how I
make my money.

**Eddie: Is that where most of your experience lies, in
Forex?**

Rob:    Yes. I started in Forex and I stayed in that industry
through all the twists and turns; regulations,
problems and broker issues. I couldn't possibly be
happier to have stayed in that industry. For all of the
problems that it has, it's really been home for me in
the world of trading, now for 14 years.

**Eddie: Once you got started, how long did it take you to
figure out how to make money?**

Rob:    A good friend, who managed about $100 million as
an investment advisor, lived 30 miles north of me. I
went to see him. Matt just has dollar signs instead
of eyeballs. He's done well for his clients and for
himself. He's the consummate risk taker, so the
opposite of Ron.

Many of us have had the experience of someone offering us money after we announce that we're going to start trading. There's no reason anybody should believe in you. Like a complete idiot, I took $2,500 from Matt, drove up to his office every day, got on his Internet connection, got on charting software, and I started following these commentaries that were posted online. Before the days of blogs and Twitter, there was a guy who posted in this forum. He said he talked to brokers, traders on the floor, and that he's had inside knowledge of, in particular, the dollar yen. I started trading the dollar yen. He would say you should buy at this level, or sell at this level, and I blindly followed his instruction.

Now, once again, Eddie, another complete rookie mistake. This guy was right. I was up 10% in my account. It was a 100% win streak and I thought I could do no wrong.

As any reasonable individual would do, I decided to massively increase my trade size on the very next trades. I remember clear as day, I was up 10% in three weeks. I was now going to massively increase my trade size so I could be up 10% every few days. The next trade I took from that person was the last trade that person ever announced, and it was absolutely incorrect. I decided I was going to hold on to that trade until the bitter end, because he had been right many times before. Maybe the market would come around. I took that account to a margin call and I ended up with $250 of that $2,500.

Ironically, with some poetic justice thrown in, I ended up left with only the profit that I had made in the last three weeks of trading. That 10%, which was a spectacular gain, just wasn't good enough for me. I blew up my first account, like many people do, and I just felt like a complete idiot. I felt more desperate than ever.

**Eddie: How long was it, from when you first started with real money to when you blew up the account?**

Rob: 24 days. Later on in my career, I was the Chief Market Strategist at a major currency broker. I did some research into the trading accounts of beginning traders that started with less than $5,000. Typically, they would lose their account in 90 days. I was even worse than the worst traders in the world. I often say, if we could all get back just two of our worst trades, think of the money that we would have.

**Eddie: What happened next?**

Rob: This is critical. I had some real breakthroughs, the first of which was that I was going to earn Matt's money back and return it to him. Then I'd be done.

Matt and I had a talk that day and I didn't know how to tell him I'd lost it all.

He'd been in the business long enough. He told me there was no way I was going to make money on my first account. "Your first trading account is always going to blow up." I confessed then. He said to me, "You think you learned your lesson, which is that you shouldn't take too much risk, but you haven't. That's going to take longer to learn." He told me the most important lesson is that there is no privacy on Wall Street. There's no way to make money and also have complete privacy.

You're either willing to talk to people about the trades you take and the mistakes you make, or you want to keep it a secret. Look at the history of Wall Street: the ones who keep their trading a secret blow everything up.

At that point, we were talking about the fund called Long-Term Capital Management, which essentially put the whole financial system on the brink of disaster by keeping a bunch of trades on the Russian ruble private. Secrecy will kill you. Matt said, "We're going to put some money back in your account and you're going to tell me everything. You're going to show me the account at the end of every day." I thought, *I hate having a boss*. The struggle: the desire to be independent vs. the desire to make a bunch of money and be transparent about it.

I had to give up the fantasy that I was going to be able to not report to anybody, do my own thing, travel anywhere, trade from the beach. I realized this was going to be a job now. 11 months later, I had grown a smaller amount of money, $1,000 into $2,000. I gradually increased. My risk got a lot of leverage available to me back then.

**Eddie: What did you do different, as far as strategy?**

Rob:    The strategy had changed completely from following somebody else's recommendations blindly, to building my own system. I had read Alexander Elder's *Trading For a Living*. I had read Tom Dorsey's *Point and Figure Charting*, on the recommendation of a broker at Hambrecht & Quist. I was doing point and figure charts on the long-term charts, by hand. Then I was doing a set of moving averages on the short-term chart. I was essentially waiting for a trend to show signs of weakness by a bunch of moving averages converging on top of each other. Then I would just trade, basically, a point and figure chart reversal after that had occurred.

I built up 11 months of experience in waiting for the trade, taking the trade small. If the trade went in my favor, I added to it. If the trade went against me, I just got out.

**Eddie: This strategy was something that you came up with just based on reading?**

Rob:   Yes.

**Eddie: Did you have any type of mentor who explained this to you?**

Rob:   No, I just read. I read everything I could get my hands on. I started with Alexander Elder's book, and then I went on to books like John Murphy's *Technical Analysis of the Financial Markets*, and I became an indicator-based counter-trend trader.

**Eddie: Interesting. This is the Rob Booker methodology.**

Rob:   I always say to people that there are many ways that people pursue this business, but one of the most effective ways is to lock yourself away with simulation software so that you can back test. You either build a trading system that has a slightly larger trade size and you stop out very quickly, or a very small trade size. There are a lot of pathways to failure in trading and there are very few, in my opinion, pathways to success, but they're very open —that pathway is complete transparency and absolute focus and dedication to one methodology.

Everything that goes wrong with trading is either because we keep something a secret, or we start fooling around with some new trading system that we don't understand.

**Eddie: You took pieces of other people's methodology to create your own. I'm very familiar with Tom Dorsey and point and figure charting. There is clearly a system in there, but it sounds like you overlaid some moving averages. Where did you grab that from?**

Rob:   I came into it. By the time I started trading, I had left the San Francisco Bay Area where I went to law school and had lost access to anybody in the industry. I was living in a small town in West Virginia. I didn't have access to anybody in the financial markets. I didn't know that you could buy a trading system. I didn't even know that you could learn a trading system from a book because the first books I bought were overviews of how indicators work. I was fascinated by moving averages.

I stumbled upon stuff and thought I'd build those things myself. *No one would think about using moving averages like this.* Of course, thousands of people had thought of it before me. I truly was operating in a vacuum. Matt invested people's money in mutual funds, so my mentor was really just an accountability partner.

Ron, in San Francisco at Bear Stearns, answered my first phone call. I never talked to Ron again. I tried to reach him when Bear Stearns blew up, but that was impossible. I didn't talk to a professional in the industry until I walked onto the trading floor of Deutsche Bank in 2007. It was a long time. I knew you needed an entry, a stop, and a profit target.

**Eddie: That's pretty amazing. So, you took that loss, you wiped out the account. Your friend re-funded you and you made $1,000. Now you're learning to gradually size up your positions. What happened from there?**

Rob:   From that point on, I literally was accountable to one person for staying true to the one trading system, which was a counter-trend trading system. As far as I knew, that was all I was ever going to do, so for the next three years all I did was trade that system. I traded that system consistently in the same way with some refinements on how long I would let an open position go against me.

We just passed through years where the currency market was incredibly volatile. I traded $2,000 into $32,600 within two years. I was doing work on the side for other people. I had never gotten licensed as an attorney, but I wrote contracts and did things on the side to support myself. Once I got to that $32,000 account size, I went back to this idea that

I'm going to take a small amount of this capital, like $10,000, out. It's mid-2003, I took $10,000 out, and I decided I would continue to play the safe game with $20,000. I would pay Matt back his money because I was pretty sure that, eventually, I was going to lose it. He was the most generous person I'd ever met; he didn't want interest, all he wanted was his principle.

I decided that I was going to be aggressive with that $10,000, and that worked out. That $10,000 grew into over $100,000 in the next 12 months.

**Eddie: What did you do differently?**

Rob:   I took bigger position sizes and I stopped out of those positions faster.

**Eddie: So, you took your losses faster.**

Rob:   I took my losses, but then the other part about that is, I didn't just ride my winners. I added to my winning trades. I piled it on. I started adding in an element of daily pivot points, for example. My trades would stay open for 24-72 hours if they were just quick losses.

If they were positive, they would stay open for two to three weeks. I would literally think that if this $10,000 went up to $90,000 and then I lost it all, I would be okay with that. I have my backup trading capital that's growing slowly. On that other account that was larger, I was reducing my position size.

Eventually, I took all of the capital out of the really risky strategy because I would have draw downs— sometimes seven losing trades in a row. Because my trade size was big, I would be pulling my account down by 25% or 30%.

**Eddie: How'd you manage those emotions?**

Rob:    I didn't grow up a starving child in Africa, but I'd had some pretty traumatic experiences in my life. Anytime I got worried about a trade, I just thought, *is this worse than what I went through as a child?* No.

I had a picture on the wall of my trading office of a castle in Italy. There's a city in Italy called L'Aquila, which means "the Eagle." It was a fortress and a prison. I used to run—when I lived in Italy when I was 20—two miles a day. Part of my run would go around that castle.

I would be running so hard, I was just throwing up. I literally didn't think I could move any further. I would keep that picture above my desk and I'd ask myself, "Do I feel like that right now?" The answer was always no. This is it. I had that $10,000, I going to grow that $10,000. I had a goal of, I think,

$150,000. If I got to $150,000, I was going to pull $140,000 and do it over again.

I got to $150,000. I pulled it all out and put it in the less risky account. I realized I couldn't justify this kind of risk. You can justify it to grow your account quickly if you've got a certain portion of your trading capital, but after a certain period time it's no longer justifiable. I began the process of building a trading system that started with smaller trade sizes with a larger amount of capital. Then I could still live off of that money and increase the size of that account.

**Eddie: Was that the moment you thought *I've really got this*?**

Rob:   Yes. I thought I knew how to trade on day one.

**Eddie: We all open with that one.**

Rob:   I realized later on that I still felt that way, I didn't really know how to trade. I know how to manage risk, and that's how you know you've arrived.

**Eddie: Do you still use that system; the accountability, the transparency?**

Rob:   I call it something different now, but yes.

**Eddie: I've never heard that before, and I think that's a very interesting approach. You come clean with**

**your trading, almost like group therapy positive feedback.**

Rob:   Absolutely. It came down to what I call the "traders contract," which is if I violate the risk management, if I violate the system's focus, or if I violate the transparency or privacy commitments, I get restricted from my trading account.

A lot of this came to fruition when I went to Deutsche Bank in 2007. I visited the trading floor and, at that point, I was trading a couple million dollars. I thought I was the King.

I went on that trading floor and found that it's a whole different ball game there. I then went to the proprietary trading desk at Wells Fargo and asked, "What's your job?" to the manager, to Darren, who managed the traders at Wells Fargo. He explained that if his traders broke the rules, he'd turn their systems off and sent them home for two days. He literally treated adult traders, who made a lot of money, like children. I realized then that you don't get to a point where you get to just do whatever you want without anybody knowing about it.

That's when it occurred to me that the added component here is that there's a consequence for me.

**Eddie: How did you set up that structure? This is the first I've heard of it, and I can think of a very large group of people—including my own students—who could benefit from this concept.**

Rob: I was blogging at the time. I was a writer and I had a book contract when I was in law school. For a variety of reasons that are ridiculous, I never finished the book, never fulfilled the contract for the novel. When I got to trading successfully, I decided to start writing and speaking about the markets in whatever terms I felt necessary. I was meeting people because I was writing about the markets. One of those people that I met was Max. We started conversing via email.

Max was just the first accountability partner that I had. That is the individual to whom I was accountable and who knew what I was doing. As time went on, that circle of individuals who could see my trading account—actually log in to my trading account and see what I was doing—would grow. These days, I run online groups, which I call "trader mastermind groups," where people link up. They get the tools and resources necessary to follow up on each other.

**Eddie: You're the moderator of these rooms?**

Rob: I'm too lazy and ridiculous to even be the moderator of those rooms. I have a Facebook group where those people meet each other and I come in once a day and post in that group but they work it out themselves. I will give you tools that you can use, but then you need to do this on your own.

**Eddie: Interesting.**

Rob: You need transparency and absolute focus. If you have those two things, if you don't veer off into other trading systems and someone else can see what you're doing, you're going to be okay. There's very little advice that you actually need to be successful.

**Eddie: In all your years of trading, what's the biggest loss you ever took?**

Rob: I took a $50,000 loss on the dollar/yen in 2004. I've had draw downs that were probably $750,000-$800,000, but a realized loss of $50,000 dollar/yen. I got into a dollar/yen trade short in the 105, 104 area. At the time, the Ministry of Finance in Japan had a habit of intervening in the markets to prop up the dollar in order to keep exports strong in Japan. Back in those days, the trade balance report was the big mover. Trade was just the major driver of all conversations related to FX.

I got stuck in a position.

It was in the account that I had smaller trade size in, and I thought I was completely protected. So, I kept the trade open and the Japanese Ministry of Finance intervened in the currency market. The dollar/yen jumped, I think it was 150 points in seconds. I took a big loss.

**Eddie: How did that compare to your $750,000 draw down, on an emotional level?**

Rob: That's a good point.

**Eddie: How long was that draw down over? That's a big number.**

Rob: That probably lasted six months, trading my way out of that position. I get over obstacles, losses, and disappointments pretty quickly. I am hopefully optimistic about everything. I get angry optimistic. When I went to the draw down I just decided that— I was trading, at that time, I think $8 million.

**Eddie: Was that all your money?**

Rob: No, that was investor money.

**Eddie: Okay.**

Rob: I was a commodities trading adviser and in the currency market. It was a 10% draw down. Numerically it was a lot of money, but percentage wise it was something that I had dealt with probably 30 or 40 times before.

I think what I've learned to do is harness my ability to withstand disappointment and temporary difficulty. I have harnessed that ability. It's the opposite, Eddie. My difficult times as a trader are when it's win after win after win. I don't appreciate that.

**Eddie: Complacency.**

Rob:   Yes. When is the exciting thing going to happen? That's why I'm constantly attempting to keep boundaries and accountability around myself, because I realize that I am drawn toward the dramatic. You've got to protect yourself from yourself.

**Eddie: Our brains are literally programmed to watch the news; look for fires, floods, earthquakes, terrorist attacks, the drama. We're attracted to it.**

Rob:   I think, this is more psychological in nature, but I am convinced that the most powerful forces in human nature are habit and familiarity. For example, a child who lives in a broken home: they still want to go home to their bedroom. You can take the child out of the broken home, but they still miss their bedroom. The drama becomes familiar to them.

The reality is that we are drawn toward what is familiar to us, regardless of whether it's good for us. That is a powerful force and that's why traders have such a hard time stopping themselves from doing something that is obviously stupid. We seek out that challenge.

**Eddie:** **It's our programming. We're drawn into it and then we get familiar with it; we almost crave it. It's a habit pattern.**

Rob: I tell traders all the time not to read a lot of trading books. Flood your mind with self-help books; flood your mind with positivity. Literally reprogram your mind to become familiar with positivity, with peace of mind and happiness. You have to reprogram your brain to overcome that natural inclination to set a ceiling on how much happiness you can possibly sustain without becoming unfamiliar.

Our only limitations are the limitations that we place on ourselves. Where do we feel uncomfortable? In the unfamiliar.

With trading, being comfortable means drawing your account back down to numbers that you feel comfortable with. You will naturally do that unless you fill your life and mind with positivity.

**Eddie:** It's a very deep concept, Rob. I sincerely hope that the people reading/listening to this get to that level, but unfortunately I think very few traders actually do.

**Rob:** I agree.

**Eddie:** A big piece of that is appreciation; learning to appreciate what you accomplish. You and I could probably talk about this for hours, but I want to change gears a little bit.

**Rob:** Absolutely.

**Eddie:** I know you do The Traders Podcast—thanks for having me on The Traders Podcast a couple of times. Besides a podcast, you have other products for traders?

**Rob:** From time to time I will do a course to teach the trading system that I use, or the strategies for reprogramming your trading brain.

**Eddie:** What's your website?

**Rob:** There's a variety of them. The easiest places to go are TradersPodcast.com and RobBooker.com.

**Eddie:** When you do these, are they live webinars?

**Rob:** I probably taught 60 live seminars all over the world, back when the currency markets were just on fire. Now I prerecord lessons and sell them for $27.

I have students from all over the world and it's not my main source of income. It's $27 and self-serve.

**Eddie: From the people who've participated in your programs, what do you think is the top question you get asked?**

Rob: "How long will it take me to start trading for a living?"

**Eddie: How do you answer that question?**

Rob: Offensively, I say it takes as long as you want to take. If you want to open up to someone else completely—who has access to turn off your trading account if you break your rules—and you want to focus on one trading system exclusively, you will begin to accumulate wealth. You want to be an accumulator.

**Eddie: What is the top question you wish traders would ask you?**

Rob: "Where can I send you $20,000?" Just kidding. I love talking to traders about inspirational material that they've found. I would love to have more conversations with traders about accountability, discipline, and hacking one's brain.

**Eddie: The truth is that most traders, in the beginning, they can't see it. They've got to get banged over the head a bunch of times to be able to get it.**

Rob: That's why two people trading the same system get different results. I don't think that trading is about the financial markets, or fundamentals, or even the charts. I just don't think that trading is about trading.

I think trading success is about being a better human. If trading is your hobby, then trading is your entertainment. If trading is your job, it's a completely different story. The market is an impossible thing to figure out. The better thing to figure out is myself. I can figure that out.

**Eddie: What do you think is the number one mistake you see traders make?**

Rob: I taught my trading system to a group of people back in 2009. I did a series of online webinars. I met up with one of the traders at an expo in Las Vegas. She told me she was confused. I asked her to tell me how her testing of her trading system went. She said it went fine, it makes money, it just doesn't produce enough trades. What that person misunderstood was whether they were looking for action or they were looking for accumulation.

Now, if you patiently accumulate, you win. I would say one of the biggest traps that traders fall into is a desire for more action when they already have something sitting in front of them that's going to produce exactly what they need.

**Eddie: Excellent answer. What would be your best piece of advice to someone who wants to learn trading?**

Rob:   I would attend an open meeting of Gambler's Anonymous and not participate. What advice would you give someone thinking about starting to smoke? You'd take them to the morgue and look at people's lungs. I would say look deep and then read Joseph Conrad's *Heart of Darkness*. You are about to descend into the world's largest legal gambling operation as a beginner.

You have one hope, and that is to tie yourself to a rope and descend into that hole with somebody that you're accountable to. The first thing you should do is go to the morgue and see the wasteland of traders who blew up. You must become familiar with the worst side of yourself. Get a system. Get a routine. Get a trading partner.

I knew a guy who started trading in 2006. He says, "I'm short the British pound," or "long the British pound." I say this is a volatile time because of thin market conditions. Over the weekend, he lost all of his money; $10,000 or $50,000. I said, "You know, beginning traders blow all of their trading capital." That was 100% of this person's trading capital.

Then he says this: "That's not all. My best friend took the same trade with me. He took his life savings, $150,000, and lost all of it. His family found him attempting to saw off his hand at the dining room table."

**Eddie: Oh my God.**

Rob:    I tell traders this story all the time. You need to become intimately familiar with the absolute pain of not protecting yourself from yourself. This isn't just playing around; it's not just $1,000. Go into this with a rock solid understanding that you're either going into this as a gambler or as an accumulator investor.

I think everyone has the potential to do something great, and this is one of those things. I am generally optimistic about the chances for people's success, conditioned upon their willingness. If this is something you're truly trying to replace your income with, don't have the impression that this is more fun than working for "The Man." There are a lot of days that I think that working for "The Man" would be a lot better than the stress I put myself through at times. It's just a job.

**Rob's Key Secrets to Remember:**

1.  Everything that goes wrong with trading is either because we keep something a secret, or we start fooling

around with some new trading system that we don't understand.

2. Accountability partners will keep you honest about your trading.

3. Flood your mind with self-help books; flood your mind with positivity.

# Howard Hazelcorn

This interview is with my greatest influence, my father, Howard Hazelcorn. Howard's Wall Street career dates back to 1955. At age 13, Howard began making regular trips to the visitor's gallery of the New York Stock Exchange to chart stocks. Howard later became a floor trader and even served on the Board of Governors for the New York Mercantile Exchange. This is the second interview I have done with my dad; the first can be found in *Market Prophets: Eddie Z's Interviews with Wall Street's Legends, Gurus, All-Starts & Hall of Famers.*

**Eddie: If you can, let's quickly go over your history in the markets. You started going down to the New York Stock Exchange when?**

Howard: I was 13 years old.

**Eddie: What year was that?**

Howard: 1955.

**Eddie: 1955. 60 years ago.**

Howard: Correct.

**Eddie: What did you do down there when you were 13?**

Howard: I used to stand in the visitor's gallery and chart the prices coming over the tape because I owned a few stocks and I was very interested in the other securities on the exchange. It wasn't very difficult to do in those days because volume on the exchange totaled usually about three million shares for the day. As the prints came by, I entered them in my chart book, made bar charts, and tried to follow the market that way.

**Eddie: Were you looking for trends back then?**

Howard: Absolutely. I had limited funds, of course; I was using my mother's account because I was too young to have an account for myself. I still remember the first couple of stocks that I bought when I was 13.

**Eddie: What stocks were they?**

Howard: Sunray Mid-Continent Petroleum, which was listed on the New York and Columbia Gas Systems.

I bought five shares of the oil company and ten shares of the gas company.

**Eddie: Did you make money on those?**

Howard: Yes, they were winners for me. I don't remember what I sold them at, but I remember that I made a little money. From then on, I spent every day at the New York Stock Exchange. I knew exactly what business I wanted to be in for a career.

**Eddie: What are the deep psychological things that you need? What does it really take to be a successful trader?**

Howard: If that's what you're going do as a profession, you have to enjoy it.

**Eddie: Do you mean commitment?**

Howard: You're totally committed, but never bet the house. Always leave yourself with a cash reserve for trading. You need to have a cash reserve for special opportunities as they arise.

I also believe that you have to find a certain group of industries that interest you. For example, you can't just buy stocks in the Dow because they are on the news. In my case, I like real estate investment trusts. I'm also involved with oil stocks, as I was an oil trader.

**Eddie: So, you believe in finding specific industries that you could focus in on?**

Howard: Absolutely. You have to find niches that you can get into. I understand about oil because I traded it for so many years, so I look at that.

**Eddie: I know that later on, of course, you became a 20+ year commodities trading veteran, and you traded on the floor of the New York Mercantile Exchange.**

Howard: Yes, from 1973-1993.

**Eddie: During those years, commodities could be very volatile. Did you have any major draw-downs during that period?**

Howard: In 1981 I had a disaster. I took a huge position in heating oil spreads. I was buying February heating oil and selling December heating oil because it had been trading publicly for two years. In the prior two years those spreads opened up a great deal. As you got towards the winter, February contracts moved up many points against December. I put on a huge position, and as we got into November the position collapsed. It was a million dollar loss in one day. Believe me, that shook me up.

It put me in a very bad position since I went through a lot of money and owed the clearing house about

$400,000 because of that day. I had to scramble to pay them off.

**Eddie: How'd you recover from that, as a trader? Emotionally?**

Howard: Very slowly. I wound up earning back the million that following year, plus about $700,000 on top. I paid back the $400,000 I owed and I came out okay. I did very well after that, being a little more careful.

If you buy a stock at $15 and it closes at $10, your cost is $10. You've lost five points, and you hear that nonsense with stock traders, "you haven't lost anything until you've sold it." Yes you have; you've lost five points.

That's why so many people lose so much money in the market.

Look at it objectively and say, "Do I want to own that stock at $10?" That's when you make a decision about what to do. You have to do that with commodities because cost is irrelevant. They're so volatile and they're so leveraged compared to how much you can lose.

I take a look at my stock accounts at the end of the day and I see I'm up or down X dollars. That's what the account is worth. What I paid for it is irrelevant. That only matters when you close out positions at the end of the year. You can't look at it as holding positions.

**Eddie: Let's talk about that, because having enough capital is one of the things that it takes to become a successful trader. What would you say to somebody new to trading about how much capital they need to trade stocks, or to trade commodities?**

Howard: To trade commodities is a different story. To trade stock, I would think you need about $100,000. You can do $50,000, but the trouble is you have to leave yourself cash for a special situation. If you're going to burn out all your cash and something good comes along, then you miss a real opportunity.

**Eddie: What does that mean, $100,000? That's all the money they have in the world and they have no job, or that's money that they can afford to lose?**

Howard: That's the money they can afford to invest and risk. If you can't risk 50% of what you're going to put up, then you're not ready.

**Eddie: Right.**

Howard: Without that money, you can't jump to opportunities when they appear. Now, another thing I think it takes to be successful is that you have to take a mid-day break unless the market is very active mid-day. Usually 12:00-1:00 is the quietest time. Walk away and clear your head. Don't answer the phone. I think you can brainwash yourself by watching the screen all day, non-stop. I think it skews you in the wrong direction.

**Eddie: What would be the top three things you need to do to be successful at trading?**

Howard: If you're using a screen, keep your eye on the TV for breaking news. Whether it's political news, international news, war news, business news, keep an eye on the business channel.

I think that new traders cannot use just one computer screen. You have to use a number of screens if you're going to follow a number of stocks, so you can see changes without having to continually update your screen to change stocks. I keep 500 stocks on my screen and I can't watch them all, but I'm getting about 40 on a screen.

**Eddie: You have quite a history on Wall Street. Your most successful period was standing in the pit trading heating oil and trading propane on the floor of the New York Merc. Can you tell us any front running stories that are just ridiculous?**

Howard: I can tell you, before we had oil on the exchange (which was 1978, it started with heating oil), I was a platinum trader, I had platinum futures contracts.

Platinum was never heavily traded, and it was always an expensive commodity. In my years there, I watched it go from $160 up to $300, back to $130, then up to over $1000.

Because there was a limited number of people who traded it, there were people who handled orders for some of the metal houses and they would be in cahoots. I used to see this all the time, with what they called local traders (individuals who traded for their own account). Someone would get an order and sell 100 contracts, which was a sizable order in platinum. They'd tip their friends off that they had 100 to sell here, and their friend would immediately sell 20 lots. Then they'd start executing his order and save the last 20 lots until they'd beaten it down. They'd sell the last 20 lots to the individual, who'd make himself a nice $2000 profit.

At some point, the local would meet him in the back room and he'd give him some cash to pay him off for doing it. This was a common occurrence mostly before oil trading became the big thing. The committees on the exchange would investigate this if they saw something that was blatant, and people would get fined for doing it, but most of the time they'd get away with it. It happened a lot in platinum before there was oil.

**Eddie:** To compare it to high frequency trading, essentially someone sees your order before it gets executed, somebody trades around it and uses it as a way to make money for themselves.

Howard: Right. Self enrichment.

**Eddie:** They would execute trades in front of your order to make themselves money, taking advantage of you. That's really what front running is.

Howard: The advantage they were taking was against other people who traded from their own account who were not in on it. It was a big disadvantage.

The guy who gave the order, he was definitely taken advantage of. It was not a legal practice, but it was done on a regular basis.

It was being done because it wasn't being monitored properly.

**Eddie:** Have you witnessed any major swindles in the pit, or even as an over-the-counter trader?

Howard: The million dollar loss I took, I believe, was a major swindle. There was an oil company that, as I was buying up all of these spreads in 1981, were the major seller. I got wiped out for the million dollars and they defaulted on a thousand contracts of heating oil and went out of business. They were so busy shorting that position to me that they never even bothered to cover it.

**Eddie: Okay. How about a swindle that didn't involve you, but that you witnessed? Wasn't there once a time, I'm remembering, when the CFTC had undercover guys standing in the pit?**

Howard: Yes, but that wasn't really a swindle.

**Eddie: What was going on with that?**

Howard: There was a time before the law was changed in the early 80's, that you could roll your income because you didn't have to mark your commodity positions to the market, and it was done mostly in gold and metals.

Let's say you bought December gold and sold February gold. Let's say you had traded commodities during that year and made $100,000. You'd buy a decent position, a spread, which would vary somewhat in gold depending on interest rates. For number's sake, December was for $200 an ounce and February was $220 an ounce. You'd go along X number for one month and short the other month. As the market went up and down, the position—if you had 100 contracts—would vary thousands of dollars. You'd be making thousands on your long position if it went up, while at the same time losing the same amount of money on your short position.

You take the position that you're losing the money in, let's say where you're losing the $100,000. You've made $100,000 trading, and you're losing $100,000 on one half of that position. At the end of the year you close out that position, buying your February short position back and selling the March or April gold position out. You've taken a physical loss, but you still have the same basic spread on.

So, you were able to roll the $100,000 from year one into year two. When the new year started, you'd unravel the position and you'd start off the year with $100,000 of profit. However, your whole income for the year was zero, even though you made $100,000. One year, I believe it was 1981, that ended.

I told a lot of people on the exchange that that was ending, but nobody believed it. I wound up paying long-term capital gain on a great deal of money. When a lot of people got stuck, interest rates were very high, and so there were people who had now rolled into 1981 with $2 million and they were now subject to full taxation at short-term capital gain.

**Eddie: They'd been rolling it for years?**

Howard: They had been rolling it for years. Say they rolled in $5 million over the past 15 years. People were going to the government saying they couldn't pay the tax on whatever it was, 30% on $5 million. So, the government gave you a deal. You could pay it off at the then-current interest rate of 20%, over three years.

**Eddie: Wow.**

Howard: A good friend of mine who passed away a few years ago wound up in that position. He had to pay 20% over three, or maybe five, years. I begged him to take his profit and pay the tax, but he didn't want to believe these things. People were so busy trading commodities that they really got stuck for a lot of money. I know someone who lost his house because of that. They took the Rolex off his wrist. How about that?

**Howard's Key Secrets to Remember:**

1. Always leave yourself with a cash reserve for new opportunities.

2. Find a certain group of industries that interest you, to invest in.

3. Traders need breaks for a clear mind.

Made in the USA
Middletown, DE
10 January 2019